# Chartism

# IN THE SAME SERIES

*General Editors: Eric J. Evans and P. D. King*

LANCASTER PAMPHLETS

# Chartism

*John K. Walton*

London and New York

First published 1999
by Routledge
11 New Fetter Lane, London EC4P 4EE

Simultaneously published in the USA and Canada
by Routledge
29 West 35th Street, New York, NY 10001

Typeset in Bembo by The Florence Group, Stoodleigh, Devon
Printed and bound in Great Britain by
Clays Ltd, St. Ives PLC

*British Library Cataloguing in Publication Data*
A catalogue record for this book is available
from the British Library

*Library of Congress Cataloging in Publication Data*
Walton, John K.
Chartism / John K. Walton.
p. cm. – (Lancaster pamphlets)
Includes bibliographical references.
1. Chartism.  I. Title  II. Series.
HD8396.W35 1999
322′.2′0941–dc21
98–43083
CIP

ISBN 0–415–09689–8

# Contents

# Time Chart

| | |
|---|---|
| *1832* | Reform Act |
| *March 1834* | Transportation of Tolpuddle Martyrs |
| *July 1834* | Poor Law Amendment Act passed |
| *1835* | Formation of Working Men's Associations and Radical Associations begins |
| *June 1836* | Formation of London Working Men's Association |
| *January 1837* | Formation of East London Democratic Association |
| *April 1837* | Glasgow Cotton Spinners' strike Refounding of Birmingham Political Union |
| *November 1837* | *Northern Star* begins to appear |
| *April 1838* | Great Northern Union formed at Leeds |
| *May 1838* | People's Charter and first National Petition published |
| *June 1838* | Northern Political Union formed at Newcastle |
| *September 1838* | Great meeting at Kersal Moor, Manchester |
| *February 1839* | General Convention of the Industrious Classes meets in London |
| *March 1839* | Anti-Corn Law League established |
| *May 1839* | Convention moves to Birmingham |
| *July 1839* | Bull Ring riots in Birmingham and arrests Convention returns to London Commons reject first National Petition |

| | |
|---|---|
| *September 1839* | Convention dissolved |
| | Proposed 'Sacred Month' (general strike) abandoned |
| *November 1839* | Newport Rising and subsequent arrests |
| *January 1840* | Abortive plans for insurrection in Bradford and Sheffield |
| *February–March 1840* | Trials of arrested Chartists |
| *July 1840* | National Charter Association set up |
| *April 1841* | National Association of the United Kingdom for Promoting the Political and Social Improvement of the People founded: the 'New Move' and O'Connor's attack on it |
| *July 1841* | General Election held |
| *August 1841* | Peel takes office |
| *April 1842* | Complete Suffrage Union conference in Birmingham; Chartist Convention meets in London |
| *May 1842* | Commons reject second National Petition |
| *August–September 1842* | Great strike in northern industrial districts, with Chartist involvement. Arrest of Chartist leaders. |
| *December 1842* | Chartist representatives meet Complete Suffrage Union in Birmingham |
| *March 1843* | Trial of Feargus O'Connor and 58 others at Lancaster |
| *September 1843* | Chartist Convention in Birmingham endorses Land Plan |
| *April 1845* | Chartist Land Co-operative Society formed |
| *September 1845* | Society of Fraternal Democrats founded |
| *June 1846* | Corn Laws repealed |
| *May 1847* | 'Ten Hours' Factory Act passes |
| *July 1847* | Whigs win General Election: O'Connor victorious at Nottingham |
| *February 1848* | Revolution in France |
| *April 1848* | Chartist Convention meets in London |
| | Kennington Common mass meeting on 10 April |
| | Commons reject and pour scorn on third National Petition |
| *May 1848* | National Assembly meets |

# Introduction

The struggle for the People's Charter is deservedly given a high profile in social and political histories of nineteenth-century Britain. The issues raised by the principled pursuit of democracy, or at least manhood suffrage, in the face of entrenched opposition through judicial repression and military force on the part of the privileged and their allies, are important enough in themselves to justify extended treatment. So are the debates over means and ends, objectives and priorities, especially when they involve arguments over the legitimacy or otherwise of parallel constitutional arrangements and the recourse to 'physical force'. But the study of Chartism also features moments of high drama when Britain came closer to revolution, and the possibility of a radically different long-term trajectory of future development, than at any point between the 1640s and the aftermath of the First World War. The peaks of social and political tension in the trade depressions of 1839, 1842 and, perhaps, 1848 deserve serious consideration in this regard. Chartism tends to be treated as a reactive movement, responding to the economic stresses of the transitional 1830s and 1840s when the troughs of the trade cycle reached apocalyptic intensity, and to disappointment and anger at the practical consequences of the Reform Act of 1832. In fact, it inherited and sustained a momentum of its own, and we need to be aware of the movement's capacity to set its own agenda and make things happen in its own right, despite the personal

1

differences, faction-fighting and contrasting priorities among its leadership, and despite arguments which suggest that it was merely the temporary extension of an existing radical agenda under special circumstances, after which those of its supporters who sustained an active interest in politics returned to their original allegiances (Winstanley, 1993; Miles Taylor, 1995).

Textbook treatments of Chartism, especially some of the older works (Hovell, 1918; Ward, 1973) tend to focus on the leadership, highlighting divisions and personal deficiencies as part of a condescending approach which emphasizes the futility of the Chartist quest and the failure of the movement to achieve its political objectives. There is a tendency to focus on the Six Points which embodied Chartist prescriptions for parliamentary reform, and to concentrate on their impracticability and their incompatibility with the political realities of the time, listing the dates at which versions of this point and that eventually became law (or their failure to do so). Such presentations tend to obscure the wider package of economic and social reforms which Chartists sought to obtain under a purged and pure system of government, and the extent to which Chartist pressure helped, in some limited measure, to bring them about in the short term. It is distorting and demeaning to present Chartism as a study in futility, incompetence and self-aggrandisement, or even (in pursuit of balance) to accept the legitimacy of the ideals and aims but end on a note of elegiac regret that such romantic aspirations were necessarily out of reach. Chartism, as the climax of a long struggle by the dispossessed and disinherited to open out the constitution to embrace their needs and protect their ways of life and standards of living, deserves to be assessed on its own terms as well as on those of the established political nation whose institutions it challenged. Chartists not only struggle against the condescension of posterity to gain a hearing outside the extensive and impressive specialized literature on the theme; they also struggled at the time against the efforts of powerful contemporaries to declare their organizations illegal, to deny them meeting-places, to curb the distribution of their news and propaganda, to break up their public meetings, to arrest and imprison their leaders, to impugn their motives, to intimidate actual supporters and frighten potential ones, and to diminish their achievements. The determined intensity with which Britain's governors allocated resources to these endeavours goes far to underline the importance of the movement and the threat it seemed to pose to the existing political and social order (Saville, 1987). These are themes of enduring relevance, and this introduction to the debates over Chartism, to the nature of the movement and to its place in the broader scheme of British history will give them due weight.

The study of Chartism has also precipitated important innovations in historical method, and acted as a focus for debates over the proper stuff and agenda of historical research and writing. Since the publication in 1959 of the influential collection of essays *Chartist Studies*, edited by Asa Briggs, one of the most fruitful approaches has been through in-depth local studies, which have sought to recover the texture of Chartist activity and the social structure of the movement's support in a variety of geographical settings. This recognition of the local roots and dimensions of national movements, and the contrasting extent and nature of their following and activities in different kinds of place, has enriched our understanding of Chartism and subsequently been carried over into many other fields. Recent studies of Liverpool and Manchester, unaccountably neglected or superficially treated in the earlier waves of place-specific research, have underlined the continuing vitality of this approach alongside more conventional biographical and thematic studies with a national remit (K. Moore in Belchem (ed.), 1992; Pickering, 1995). Local studies have been an obvious vehicle for attempts, within a Marxist tradition, to test the extent to which Chartism might be regarded as an expression of working-class consciousness: a collective awareness of common interests and shared exploitation as wage-earners which pulls together working people in a variety of trades against the employing and property-owning classes, not only in trade union action but also in political campaigns (Foster, 1974). Work in this vein has raised more questions than it has answered, especially where researchers have differed over basic aspects of economic arrangements in the same locality, as in the enduring controversy over whether large or small employers dominated the economy of the test-case 'cotton town' of Oldham (Gadian, 1978; Sykes, 1980; Winstanley, 1993) but also where the nature of relationships between strikes and overtly political campaigning has been disputed (Musson, 1976; Jenkins, 1980) Nevertheless, the debates stimulated by such studies have been valuable, although this kind of agenda has been sidelined by more recent intellectual fashions, in which Chartism has also played a formative part.

3

Chartism has been the vehicle for introducing the so-called 'linguistic turn' into the mainstream of historical debate in Britain. A pioneering chapter by Gareth Stedman Jones argued that what mattered to understanding Chartism was not so much the economic conditions under which it germinated and flourished, as the approach through local studies tended to assume, but rather the language within which Chartist demands and debate were couched. This was inherited from previous radical traditions, and imprisoned Chartist notions of common sense within a rhetoric which was directed primarily against the political corruption of the aristocratic state. The expectation that the state could not be reformed short of root and branch constitutional change, and that no mitigation of the oppressive laws under which wage-earners and small traders laboured was possible without the Charter, made it impossible for Chartism to cope with the reforms of the 1840s which ameliorated conditions and redressed grievances under the existing arrangements. The language of Chartism determined what was thinkable, and when political developments undermined its assumptions and contradicted its expectations the Chartists were left devoid of effective arguments (Stedman Jones, in Epstein and Thompson (eds), 1982; Stedman Jones, 1983). This position has been challenged by Kirk, who finds alternative languages within Chartism which emphasize attacks on the economic system, together with the advocacy of a kind of socialism, and also reasserts more generally the primacy of economically based explanations over those which assume that language is the prime mover in historical explanation (Kirk, 1987). These exchanges have fed into a much wider debate about the nature of social history. While all this has been going on, Joel Wiener's biography of the Chartist leader William Lovett has emphasized the need to remember the importance of the part played by prominent individuals in shaping the movement, reviving an earlier tradition of Chartist biographies (alongside James Epstein's fuller attempt at rehabilitating the much-abused Feargus O'Connor), drawing attention to the enduring importance of the rift between Lovett and O'Connor, and reminding us that a preoccupation with language or social structure should not blind us to the importance of personalities in the working out of great historical themes (Wiener, 1989; Epstein, 1982). Chartism's place at the core of some of the most important and highly charged arguments about the philosophy of history is a further indication of

4

the topic's lively centrality to historical discussion, and in the same way arguments over the reasons for Chartism's decline require the comparative assessment of various kinds of cause and influence, under circumstances where conclusions will be affected by the historian's disposition to give more weight to some kinds of evidence and argument than to others.

Chartism is thus important not only as a subject in its own right, although its status as a critical moment and potential turning-point in modern British history is undeniable. It is also significant in terms of the ways in which historians have written about it. The analysis of Chartism which follows will take account of both dimensions. It will begin in Chapter 1 with an outline of the trajectory of the movement, with due attention to background and antecedents, and especially to a context which brought together economic and political grievances among growing numbers of the politically disenfranchised. The timing and nature of Chartism's decline will also be addressed. The argument will move on in Chapter 2 to look at the aims of the Chartists, and the extent to which the Charter was a means to other ends, using this analysis to explain why Chartism was stronger in some regions and kinds of place than in others, and to explore the extent to which it was able to attract, and retain, middle-class as well as working-class support. A third chapter will examine the strategies of the Chartists, paying heed to the dominant strands within the movement and examining the vexed question of recourse to 'physical force' or 'ulterior measures'. The extent to which Chartism was ever interested in posing, or able to pose, a plausible 'threat of revolution' will be discussed here, as will the question of the relationship between the rhetoric and language used by Chartists and the policies and priorities of the movement. Responses to Chartism from above will be examined in a fourth chapter, both in terms of legal coercion and military repression, and of the redress of grievances through the passing of legislation and the softening of existing policies. A fourth and final chapter will assess the reasons for and significance of the rise and fall of the movement in relation to the conflicting philosophies of history which have been brought to bear. But we begin by presenting the movement's story and setting.

# 1
# Chartism in Outline

## The Nature of the Charter

The People's Charter was officially launched on 8 May 1838. Its Six Points were directed at the opening out and purification of the constitution through reform of the procedures for choosing members of the House of Commons. Thus the extension of the vote to all men over 21 years of age expressed the democratic principle, while the secret ballot was intended to emancipate voters from the corrupting influences of bribery, coercion and intimidation. Accountability was pursued through the proposal for the renewal of MPs' mandates through annual elections, in an attempt to ensure that parliamentary life did not divorce them from the legitimate concerns of their constituents. The democratisation of Commons membership as well as electoral processes was envisaged. This was to be encouraged by the abolition of the property qualification to stand for parliament, which was to be replaced by the gathering of signatures from at least a hundred local electors, and the payment of a salary (of a substantial £500 per annum) to MPs, which would enable working-class representatives to serve in parliament and free them from potentially corrupting financial patronage from wealthy or governing interests. The sixth point, the introduction of electoral districts of equal size in population terms, not only did away with tiny constituencies which could be dominated by individuals but, more generally, proposed to replace the existing logic by which the Commons was said to represent property and interests with a democratic, statistically minded understanding of how the will of the people should be embodied in the legislature (Ward, 1973 pp. 84–5).

It is interesting to see what was not included in this emblematic core of the Chartist programme: no mention of the House of Lords, for example, despite the anti-aristocratic rhetoric inherited from earlier critiques of the constitution which reverberated though the movement, and the proposals for abolishing or radically reforming the Lords which had emanated from Daniel O'Connell, Francis Place and J.A. Roebuck, for example, in the mid-1830s; no overt challenge to the Crown (although some Chartists were also republicans); and no attempt to bring women back into the pale of the constitution after their exclusion had been confirmed in 1832, although this latter theme was at times a source of animated discussion. Anna Clark has argued that this disabled Chartists rhetorically, because they failed to follow through the logic of their position that full citizenship including the vote was a 'universal political right of every human being', to include female suffrage, while making themselves vulnerable to ridicule from political opponents who highlighted that logic and argued that the Chartists would be bound by it, with what were widely assumed to be absurd and dangerous consequences (Vernon (ed.), 1996 p. 235). Chartism thus suffered the worst of both worlds on this issue, failing to get the full credit for its democratic assumptions but being tarred with the brush of sentimental impracticality by opponents who assumed that being female, or indeed not being master of a household, was an automatic badge of irresponsibility and disqualification from the vote.

The irony of this was that the Charter attempted to avoid giving such hostages to fortune, pursuing practical politics, but at the level of the working of the system: specific reforms and redresses of grievances would follow from the changing composition and concerns of a reformed parliament. Its demands were limited accordingly, and its creators maintained the fixation on the reform of the House of Commons which had sustained more than two generations of radical reformers. This meant that not only would the Charter itself have to be achieved through the existing parliament's acceptance of the overwhelming moral force of the document's innate rightness; the political gains which were supposed to flow from it would also depend on recognition by the other elements of the constitution, the House of Lords and the Crown, that the democratic mandate of the Commons conferred a special legitimacy which had to be respected when controversial legislation emerged from the reformed House. This was assumed rather than discussed at the time, and was part of an optimistic set of expectations which flowed from the established language and assumptions of the culture of radical reform.

The Charter emerged from a widespread disaffection with the 1832 settlement which had been generating protest meetings and radical programmes in various parts of the country from the earliest days of the first post-Reform parliament. Already in September 1832 Birmingham's Committee of the Unemployed Artisans was advocating universal suffrage, the ballot, annual parliaments and the abolition of the property qualification (Behagg, in Epstein and Thompson (eds), 1982 p. 63). In April 1833 London's National Union of the Working Classes, which had been founded in 1831, was publicizing William Lovett's advocacy of the same measures. A month later a gathering at Padiham, in the Lancashire weaving district, came up with five of what were to become the Six Points; the Radical Association of Leeds made similar demands in 1835 (Ward, 1973 pp. 74–5, 89). Examples could be multiplied up and down the country. The Charter was the particular form in which the agenda of the radical reformers of the 1830s came to be embodied: it proved to be a very effective rallying-point, but there was nothing sacred or inevitable about its precise content, which reflected widespread current concerns. Its immediate genesis in 1837–8 came from the London Working Men's Association (LWMA), an organization of the capital's self-conscious artisan elite which set a premium on education and mutual improvement. The LWMA was distanced considerably from the ferment of provincial agitation (against the New Poor Law of 1834 and other threatening measures of the post-Reform governments) which was to provide the backbone of so much Chartist support. The credit for the actual wording and content of the Charter was disputed between William Lovett of the LWMA and the ubiquitous veteran London radical Francis Place, but what mattered was the timing of the initiative rather than the precise wording or even content of the text. Along with the LWMA, the Charter was signed by a group of parliamentary radicals led by the Irish leader Daniel O'Connell, who was no friend to unorthodox economic measures, and still less to trade unions, for example; and the influence of Place, who was a complete convert to the rising orthodoxies of free-market economics, helped to ensure that no hint of challenge to recent economic 'reforms', even the New Poor Law itself, would be allowed to compromise a purely political agenda. As John Belchem remarks (Belchem, 1990 p. 104), 'The Charter was a moderately phrased statement of the traditional radical programme.' It was only the surrounding circumstances that turned it into an icon of political and economic dissent.

## Origins of the Charter

The Charter caught on in the provinces, and became the basis for a national movement only when it was linked to the Birmingham Political Union's (BPU) campaign for one last great petition to parliament for manhood suffrage, coupled with the election of a National Convention or popular alternative parliament to organize its presentation. The BPU's original panacea was currency reform, aiming at expanding the money supply to increase popular purchasing power, demand and employment. It had pursued this agenda vigorously during the campaign leading up to the Reform Act, but this specific goal, the product of the banker Thomas Attwood's theories, was soon sidelined in the new agitation, while the scepticism of many of the BPU's middle-class leaders about universal suffrage was temporarily laid aside (Behagg, in Epstein and Thompson (eds), 1982 p. 67). The petition embodied only five of the six points of the Charter, because Attwood drew the line at equal electoral districts, but it lay at the core of subsequent campaigning (Mather, 1980 p. 10). Both the BPU and the LWMA were in touch with networks of sister organizations across the country, the inheritance of two generations of reform campaigns; and at the beginning of June 1838, at a meeting on Hunslet Moor on the outskirts of Leeds, Feargus O'Connor's Great Northern Union brought together in loose federation an array of local radical associations in Lancashire and Yorkshire whose strong language and forceful demeanour came more directly out of the frustrations of grappling with post-1832 parliaments over the Poor Law and factory reform.

There was some rivalry between the various spheres of influence. The northern group around O'Connor, and his London allies in the Marylebone Radical Association (which dated from

1835), were initially suspicious of the Charter's immediate origins. Its progenitors were held to be too closely associated with Whig reformers who were tainted with the memory of the compromise or betrayal of 1832, and with Malthusian doctrines which blamed poverty on fecklessness and early, 'improvident' marriage and sought to restrain population growth and poor relief expenditure. But there was also much overlap. The crucial point was the extent to which local campaigns, many of which involved experienced activists and well-established radical groups who had campaigned on many previous issues and occasions, were finding common ground in pursuit of shared goals whose achievement was seen to depend on national political reform. Chartism built on established cultures of radical reform, whose deep roots were a strength, although the personal antagonisms and local jealousies which had emerged over the years could also be a hindrance.

What attracted enthusiastic support was the Charter itself, and the stirring (although far from novel) ways of moving towards it which were being envisaged. When O'Connor's recently founded *Northern Star*, with its charismatic editor and established commitment to the campaigns for factory reform and against the new Poor Law, took up the cause with enthusiasm, the picture was complete. The importance of the *Northern Star* in distributing arguments, rhetoric and information, offering justifications and affirming strength, commitment and a sense of community across a wide area, was such that Dorothy Thompson has suggested that it makes more sense to date Chartism's origins from the foundation of the paper in November 1837 than from the actual publication of the Charter itself (D. Thompson, 1984 p. 6). This may be contentious, and although the *Star* remained pre-eminent, a broader Chartist press with many regional and local outlets was already proliferating in 1838 (Ward, 1973 p. 108); what is clear is that by the late spring and early summer of that year a lively and assertive movement had been born, providing a common banner under which a variety of existing causes, grievances and organizations could be marshalled, and fusing together potentially contradictory elements (embracing, for example, the full spectrum of views on political economy and of religious attachment, and bringing representatives of employers and workpeople into uneasy alliance) in pursuit of a common political goal. How it was to be achieved, and what was to be done with it if success were attained, remained highly problematic and divisive issues.

## The Convention and the First Petition

As industrial England moved into one of the severest trade depressions of the century, and the fiercely contested administrative
introduction of the New Poor Law continued, the work of
collecting signatures for the great petition, and setting up and
sustaining the Convention, went ahead during 1838 and on into
1839. It was accompanied and reinforced by a quickening rhythm
of theatrically presented open-air mass meetings whose scale,
symbolism and oratory conjured up the possibility of armed
conflict and revolution, thoroughly alarming those in authority.
Nocturnal meetings by the flaring light of smoking torches, at
which flamboyant speakers issued dark and graphic hints of the
consequences if Parliament were to reject the petition, provoked
flurries of special anxiety until a worried government declared
them illegal in December 1838. They were abandoned, but only
after a final show of defiance with valedictory meetings at
Wakefield and Bury (Epstein, 1982 pp. 119–23). The excluded
were mobilizing to claim their constitutional rights, and they
were marshalling in at least as disciplined a way as in 1819 though
in even greater numbers and with a broader agenda of potential
change, which for many supporters went far beyond the letter
of the Charter itself.

The delegates to the General Convention of the Industrious
Classes had been elected by mass meetings during the summer
and autumn of 1838. The great northern gatherings at Kersal
Moor, Manchester, on 25 September and at Peep Green, between
Leeds and Huddersfield, on 15 October, attracted crowds which
were estimated at a quarter of a million or more, and the Kersal
Moor meeting retained its enthusiasm through a heavy rainstorm
(Gammage, 1969 pp. 59–66). Arrangements were made to collect
a 'National Rent' from the localities to fund its operations. Such
a body was not a new idea: indeed, as Dorothy Thompson points
out, 'British parliamentary reform had been organized around the
idea of an alternative Parliament since the middle of the eighteenth century', and the ill-fated Peterloo meeting in 1819 had
been part of a similar process (D. Thompson, 1984 p. 63). There
were exciting overtones of the French Revolution about such a
process, but it also harked back to English constitutional precedents in 1660 and 1689 when bodies with the same label met to
restore the monarchy. Every effort was made to deprive the

11

authorities of any semblance of a legitimate excuse for dissolving this alternative legislature by force, despite its provocative role as an 'anti-Parliament' which challenged the higher legitimacy of the existing body (Epstein, 1982 p. 138). This was difficult, because the legal position was problematic: as Dorothy Thompson puts it, 'A central meeting of mandated delegates would certainly have been illegal under the Seditious Meetings legislation. However, by calling the meeting the General Convention of the Industrious Classes, carefully avoiding the expression "National Convention", by having the delegates chosen by acclamation at public meetings and by limiting the number of delegates to forty-nine, the Chartist leaders hoped to keep within the law' (D. Thompson, 1984 p. 64). Even so, the formal legality of the Convention remained questionable, and it operated under the perpetual shadow of forcible dissolution and mass arrests. The obvious inequity of these limitations went far to outweigh the necessary loss of democratic credentials which the mode of election occasioned in the eyes of some later historians.

The Convention's members gathered to begin their deliberations in London on 4 February 1839, meeting originally at the British Coffee House in Cockburn Street. As originally constituted it was a very respectable-looking body, dominated numerically by businessmen, professionals and shopkeepers rather than by manual workers. At least 39 of the original 63 delegates listed by James Epstein fall squarely into one of these categories, including lawyers, surgeons, merchants, a Unitarian minister and a clergyman of the Church of England. Some were marginal members of what R.S. Neale has called the 'middling class', working men who had moved into insecure small businesses, sometimes as a refuge from victimization for radical and trade union activities; but there was a core of solid middle-class representatives, especially the Birmingham merchants and master manufacturers of the BPU (Epstein, 1982 pp. 142–4; Neale, 1968). But there was a strong leavening of manual workers, such as the weaver Richard Marsden from Preston, although its extent was limited by the danger of losing one's job and being victimized and blacklisted by employers thereafter (King, 1981; Epstein, 1982 pp. 139–40; Kemnitz, 1978). Working men's circumstances persistently made Chartism dependent for its leadership, beyond the localities, on radical businessmen and professionals who could afford the time and cope with the disruption which a full-time delegate's role entailed.

From the beginning, the purpose of the Convention's deliberations was problematic. When its members gathered, the Petition still had only half a million signatures and there was debate over whether to send out 'missionaries' to agitate the localities in pursuit of a more impressive muster. Fifteen were sent out, despite fears of illegality, but met with limited success in areas where Chartism had lacked spontaneous support (Epstein, 1982 p. 147; Ward, 1973 p. 118). Meanwhile, the Convention debated a variety of issues, but the key question was whether it should go beyond merely presiding over the presenting of the Petition, and consider what was to be done if – or when – it was rejected by the Commons. A formal proposal to confine activities to organizing the Petition was rejected by 36 votes to 6, and the Convention began to consider the 'ulterior measures' which might be adopted to intimidate the Government into reconsidering a rejection. In May 1839 the suggested options were published as the 'Manifesto of Ulterior Measures', which contained the famous phrase that the poor would prevail against their oppressors 'peaceably if we may, forcibly if we must'. Several possibilities were outlined to make the Government's position untenable: withdrawing funds from savings banks; converting paper money into gold or silver (a ploy reminiscent of the campaign for reform in 1830–2); a general strike or 'national holiday' lasting for a 'sacred month' to bring the economy to its knees; the use of armed force to defend the people against injustice; the support of Chartist candidates at elections; abstaining from consuming articles from which government derived revenue through excises; refusal to pay rents and taxes; and 'exclusive dealing', the boycotting of traders whose politics were adversarial to Chartism (Wiener, 1989 pp. 65–6; Ward, 1973 p. 122; Gammage, 1969 p. 109). By the time this document was discussed, the Convention had moved from London to Birmingham: arrests of Chartist leaders had begun and a provincial venue, with plenty of assertive popular support and (as some delegates pointed out) a centre for arms manufacture, was deemed safer than the capital. Debate on the 'ulterior measures' was fierce, and a decision on which should be given priority was remitted to a series of simultaneous mass meetings on Whit Monday, which also provided an opportunity for a show of numerical strength and enthusiasm. The Convention adjourned until 1 July, when it would reconvene to watch over the actual presentation of the petition to the adjourned House of Commons.

Meanwhile, it surrendered the initiative to the mass meetings of the Whitsuntide holiday.

## Repression and the Threat of Insurrection

Over the three months of its meetings the Convention itself had changed. It had lost the supporters of J.P. Cobbett, who had tried to insist on a purely petitioning role, and then the Birmingham manufacturers of the BPU, whose departure at the end of March was an alarmed reaction to the violence of some of the rhetoric. The replacements for these 'respectable' members were almost all working men: a silversmith, a stonemason, a bricklayer, a framework knitter (Epstein, 1982 p. 144). The solidly middle-class Birmingham men had not been averse to bringing pressure to bear on the government by encouraging mass agitation but control of events had passed into other hands, and they were not prepared to subordinate themselves to artisan or working-class radicals of a different stamp. Their departure gave more weight to the group which Dorothy Thompson has described as the 'Jacobins', who deployed the rhetoric and symbolism of the French Revolution and envisaged an armed rising as a genuine possibility: G.J Harney wore a red 'cap of liberty', waved daggers before audiences and compared himself with the notoriously bloodthirsty French revolutionary Jean-Paul Marat. Their expectations were widely shared among Convention delegates as the spring of 1839 gave way to summer, and even William Lovett, later regarded as a moderate apostle of 'moral force', shared in a language of threatened violence which was 'in the air' across a wide range of delegates at the time. This both encouraged and responded to a swelling current of support for direct action among Chartists in the localities, and especially in the industrial towns and villages of northern and midland England (Ward, 1973 p. 117; Gammage, 1969 p. 107; D. Thompson, 1984 pp. 65–6; Wiener, 1989 pp. 64, 68).

Even as some of the more cautious middle-class elements left the Convention, it faced the problem of how to satisfy the thirst for strong and physical measures which had long been widespread among the rank and file. The delay in presenting the Petition, after parliament had been adjourned in the spring, worsened the problem. In Lancashire and the West Riding of Yorkshire especially, evidence that working people were acquiring arms was widespread and well known to Chartist leaders from the anti-New Poor Law origins of the movement in 1838, and in early 1839 blacksmiths were making pikes (a weapon which conjured up associations with both the English and the French revolutions) for distribution to their neighbours in the Lancashire cotton district. There was also evidence of arming in the Newcastle area and in South Wales (Sykes, 1985; D. Thompson, 1984 pp. 196–8; Epstein, 1982 p. 175). Speakers at the Convention were eager to emphasize the legality of such activities by displaying historical precedents for the right of the citizen to bear arms, and emphasizing the way in which the authorities were building up their forces through the new police, spy systems and the deployment of the army (Jones, 1975 pp. 149–50). Such aspirations and fears had to be met with appropriate rhetoric (without going over the uncertain boundary into 'seditious libel' and other vague but menacing categories of crime), without precipitating an actual outbreak before due constitutional procedures had been exhausted, and without any hope of success against a well-organized government. This was the tightrope which the Convention had to walk (Epstein, 1982 pp. 170–82).

The simultaneous Whitsuntide meetings were themselves a challenge to authority, aimed at gathering large crowds which would stretch the resources of police and army. The expectation of repression was strong, especially as arrests of Convention delegates and the suppression of public meetings had already taken place. Such an outcome was both feared and hoped for, as it might set off a spontaneous defensive insurrection against a government which had moved beyond the legal sphere by attacking legally constituted assemblies. The Lord Lieutenant of the West Riding of Yorkshire was invited to convene the Peep Green meeting, to add extra opprobrium to any subsequent attempt to put it down, but he refused to do so. In the event, the meetings passed off peacefully, with attendances of upwards of 400,000 reported (no doubt optimistically) at Blackwood, Monmouthshire, the gathering-point for industrial South Wales; 200,000 claimed at Kersal Moor and Peep Green, with a strong military presence; and well over 100,000 at Newcastle upon Tyne and on successive evenings at Glasgow Green. Many smaller places attracted gatherings estimated in five figures, such as the 50,000 at Sunderland, and the impressions given were imposing even if the statistics were somewhat creative (Gammage, 1969 pp. 109–22).

As the Convention reconvened in Birmingham in early July 1839, the local magistrates stepped in to use force against a series of Chartist meetings which had been held in the town's Bull Ring, partly at the behest of shopkeepers who claimed damage to their trade. William Scholefield, the Mayor and a former council member of the BPU, brought in 60 of the hated metropolitan police, symbols of central government power, to do so. Violent resistance led to arrests in a full-scale riot on 4 July, when soldiers were brought in to rescue the police; and in the aftermath four members of the Convention were arrested. Disturbances continued for several days as Chartist meetings were attacked in other parts of the town, and the episode culminated in the burning of shopkeepers' stock in the streets. Chartist meetings across the country defended the right of public assembly (Behagg, in Epstein and Thompson, (eds), 1982 pp. 80–1; Gammage, 1969 pp. 131–8). The Birmingham author-ities' actions, which marked an end to the early phase of collaboration between the 'productive classes' for reform in the town, looked like the beginning of sustained state repression against the Convention, which moved to London to wait for the Commons' response to the Petition. It proved to be a false alarm at this stage, although arrests of Chartist leaders continued; but it helped to firm up the Convention's resolve to advocate adop-tion of the 'sacred month', a potentially revolutionary step which had hitherto been regarded with misgivings, not least because the readiness and willingness of the workers to follow this path remained uncertain. Among activists, there was increasingly apocalyptic belief in impending revolution, but the extent of this in the wider world had yet to be shown (Epstein, 1982 pp. 170–3)

In the midst of all this, the Petition was at last considered by the Commons, under the sponsorship of Thomas Attwood of Birmingham and the Todmorden cotton master and factory reform campaigner John Fielden. The work of collecting signa-tures had continued throughout the spring and summer, and the final tally was 1,280,000; but this made little difference to the Commons, which rejected consideration of the Charter by 235 votes to 46 on 12 July 1839 (D. Thompson, 1984 p. 69 – her version of the vote excludes two tellers on each side; Gammage, 1969 p. 143). This left the Convention to decide how to respond. Before the Birmingham confrontations it had been discussing 'ulterior measures' but the dominant opinions at that time put other, less immediately threatening options ahead of the 'sacred month'. The developments of the first half of July raised fears and expectations among local activists and precipitated a shift in attitudes; the 'sacred month' was adopted, in the knowledge that it might lead to a revolutionary uprising, and on 16 July the Convention approved Robert Lowery's motion that it should begin on 12 August, after rejecting proposals from the insurrectionary left that it should start immediately. But this was the high point of the Convention's resolve, and it soon began to retreat from the plan as it became apparent that impending trade depression and large stocks of manufactured goods awaiting sale would negate the economic impact of the strike, and while delegates from the most militant and well-organized areas admitted to uncertainty about the real extent of practical support. After a fortnight of agonizing, the 'sacred month' was reduced and diluted to three days of strikes and meetings, and the eager warriors in the industrial districts, with their caches of arms, complained of betrayal. But even the most outspoken of the leadership, including Feargus O'Connor himself, feared the consequences of taking on the army in an unprepared and disorganized condition. The military commanders in the most disaffected areas privately feared the consequences of even a single defeat for their men, and it seemed that a single spark might provoke a conflagration even without the Convention's backing; but it was not to be. This was an ignominious defeat: the Convention could move neither backwards nor forwards, and on 6 September it dissolved itself, leaving a ferment of anger and dissatisfaction in the districts which had been preparing themselves for what they hoped would be the final conflict (Epstein, 1982 pp. 171–86).

As Chartist leaders were picked off one by one through arrest and incarceration, especially during the three days of meetings and demonstrations that marked the remnant of the 'sacred month', talk of armed uprising persisted in many industrial districts (D. Thompson, 1984 pp. 73–4). The summer and autumn of 1839, as the depression began to bite, were dangerously turbulent, and the authorities remained vigilant. Groups within the movement had effectively gone 'underground', and members of the insurrectionary wing such as Dr John Taylor and Bradford's 'Fat Peter' Bussey began to plot armed uprisings. The most

17

dramatic chain of events occurred at and around Newport, in South Wales, on the night of 3–4 November, when several thousand men from the Welsh mining and ironworking valleys marched on the town to try to take control of it. The leaders included John Frost, a linen draper, former Mayor of Newport, Convention member and a former magistrate (removed from office for his defiant radical utterances). The invaders were beaten off by troops firing from the Westgate Hotel, with the loss of at least 22 lives, and the dispersal of the workers' army was followed by a wave of arrests. Frost and two others were sentenced to death for high treason. The wider significance of this episode, which showed how deeply feelings ran among the working class in the raw and independent new industrial settlements of the Valleys, is difficult now to judge, not least because at the trials the Chartists' lawyers were at pains to reduce the gravity of the charge by labelling the episode as a mere riot rather than a full-scale insurrection. But it appears that the rising was based on a well-established network of Chartist cells, meeting in beerhouses and keeping their counsel, and that the fall of Newport was intended to be a signal for other risings elsewhere, especially in south Yorkshire. The failure of the attack provided dispiriting confirmation of the impossibility of taking on the army in an isolated campaign, while exposing the myth that British troops would not open fire under such circumstances. Subsequent smaller attempts at insurrection, which continued into January 1840 and were aimed partly at saving or avenging Frost, met with a similar though less dramatic and evocative fate, and in at least one case a government agent had infiltrated the conspirators; indeed, spies were infiltrating meetings in significant numbers from the Bull Ring riots in July 1839 onwards. The failure of petitioning had been followed by the more ignominious failure of physical force (Charlton, 1997 pp. 20–7; D. Thompson, 1984 pp. 79–87; David Jones, 1985; Wilkes, 1984; Behagg, in Epstein and Thompson (eds), 1982 p. 81).

## Rebuilding the Movement: the National Charter Association

As Dorothy Thompson argues, the year 1839 alone would need a whole fat volume in a full-scale study of Chartism (D. Thompson, 1984 p. 73). It was a year of high hopes and

18

aspirations, sadly extinguished; and the levels of commitment and mass support which were reached in the spring and summer were never to be attained again. As Epstein remarks, the beginning of 1840 marked a turning point and change of tone: 'Never again would Chartism quite recapture the widespread conviction that the achievement of working-class political power was within its immediate grasp, or the feeling of a mass willingness to risk all in a final confrontation to overthrow corrupt government and a system of economic and social oppression' (Epstein, 1982 p. 209). Even in the years of Chartist revival in 1842 and 1848, the circulation of the *Northern Star* never averaged more than one-third of the 36,000 weekly sales (with a very large number of readers per copy) that it achieved in 1839 (Mather, 1980 p. 11). But there was enough resilience and determination for the movement to rebuild itself from the grassroots, finding its immediate goal in a fierce determination to save the lives of Frost, Williams and Jones, the Newport leaders who faced the death penalty. The campaign to save them, based on a petition to the Queen which drew fervent support, revived the apparent validity of this tactic, especially when the outcome seemed to be successful. At the beginning of February 1840 the death sentences were reduced to transportation for life, and although the petitioning campaign seems not to have been the main reason for the outcome, this sign that the government was open to moral pressure and not completely intransigent took some of the heat out of the conflict. It may have helped to quell further insurrectionary stirrings. At the same time, however, a succession of Chartist leaders stood trial and were sentenced for their words and actions (often misrepresented) at the climax of the agitation, and in May 1840 O'Connor himself was sentenced to eighteen months' imprisonment after a trial at York in which he seized every opportunity to make Chartist propaganda. But from these endings came new beginnings (Epstein, 1982 pp. 208–12).

The summer of 1840 saw the emergence of a more systematic, even bureaucratic structure of Chartist organization, firmly founded in the localities. Such a system would have been useful to harness the enthusiasm of the previous year. The National Charter Association (NCA), founded in Manchester in July 1840, had a 22-point constitution which divided the membership into classes of ten whose leaders fed into ward, town, 'county and riding' and national councils. It provided for the payment of key officials, the registration of members and the collection and use of subscriptions, and it urged constitutional means by which the 'great end' of the Charter might be advanced, enjoining sobriety on the membership in the process (Jones, 1975 pp. 195–200; D. Thompson, 1971 pp. 288–93). There is scope for argument over whether this system owed more to trade union, Methodist or parish government experience and precedent. Charlton claims that 'the model was a trade union one', but without any direct supporting evidence, although it did have affinities with trade union modes of organization with which many Chartists were certainly familiar (Charlton, 1997 p. 28; Sykes, in Epstein and Thompson (eds), 1982). But many Chartists had also experienced Methodist ways of organizing, which had a broader impact on the movement: 'Class meetings, weekly subscriptions, hymns, camp meetings and Love Feasts were all employed by Chartists' (Hempton, 1984 p. 211). Eileen Yeo put this in perspective by showing that Chartism, unlike Wesleyan Methodism, safeguarded popular control through the election of class leaders, and she also pointed out that another affinity could be drawn between Chartist organization and the parish system of local government, where the quarterly meetings of the vestry had been attracting increasing popular participation in the early nineteenth century (Yeo, in Epstein and Thompson (eds), 1982 pp. 353–60; Fraser, 1976 pp. 24–36). This was, in any case, a commonsense way of organizing, as was reflected in parallel developments in Owenism, friendly societies and trade unions at about the same time, and perhaps not too much should be read into these competing explanations for its roots (Epstein, 1982 p. 226; Belchem, 1990 pp. 111–14). More important were the constraints which were imposed by the surviving legislation of the 1790s against corresponding societies. Opponents of the NCA, who also feared the centralization of power in such a body and the opportunities afforded to the authorities by keeping a central register of members, played the 'illegality' card, and an enduring sense of vulnerability was expressed in subsequent changes in the system by the NCA to emphasize that all belonged to one society rather than the federation of local bodies to which the laws objected. Fears of illegality kept prominent Chartists like William Lovett and John Collins out of the NCA (Epstein, 1982 p. 227).

After a slow start, which probably owed something to such reservations, the NCA grew rapidly and spread outwards from its original heartland in Lancashire and the West Riding of Yorkshire. In February 1841 it still contained only 80 local associations, but by the end of that year the number had grown to 282, with 20,000 members. NCA election results from 83 localities in June 1841 suggested only about 5,000 active participants, but a petitioning campaign for the return of Frost from transportation had already produced two million signatures, and too much should not be read into the limited electoral involvement (Ward, 1973 p. 145). By June 1842 there were over 400 local associations and 50,000 members, although what proportion of these were up-to-date with their subscriptions is uncertain. Membership probably peaked in autumn 1842, when over 70,000 membership cards had been issued, although, again, it is not clear how many were still current. On the basis of membership cards taken out between March 1841 and October 1842 the NCA's strongholds were in the Lancashire cotton towns (with 2,800 in Manchester itself and an impressive 350–400 in little Clitheroe, whose membership outnumbered much larger places like Preston and Stalybridge); the West Riding textile district around Leeds and especially Bradford, while Hebden Bridge, also surrounded by small weaving settlements, almost matched Clitheroe's showing; Sheffield, which counted 2,000 members; the centres of the footwear and hosiery trades in the East Midlands, from Sutton-in-Ashfield to Northampton; the Staffordshire Potteries; the Black Country in the West Midlands; the north-eastern coalfield around Newcastle upon Tyne; the South Wales valleys; and the towns of the West Country from Gloucester to Trowbridge, where there were also declining craft industries (including footwear at Bath, which shared with Cheltenham and Brighton the unexpected distinction of combining a high-class resort and residential economy with a strong and enduring Chartist presence). There was also a growing presence in London itself, where 8,000 membership cards were issued. Scotland did not embrace the NCA, having developed a different set of institutions of its own, and the membership figures formed only the tip of the iceberg, with many committed Chartists being unable to afford or to keep up the small subscriptions, or holding themselves aloof from the increasingly O'Connorite politics of the NCA, or simply scornful of this system of organization, preferring to celebrate spontaneity and independence (Epstein, 1982 pp. 229–33; Neale, 1981).

The NCA nevertheless offered a structure and organizational spine which had hitherto been lacking in Chartism. It also provided a focal point for the social lives of active members: as Belchem comments, 'The NCA was the cornerstone of a democratic counter-culture of Chartist schools, stores, chapels, burial clubs, temperance societies, and other facilities for education, recreation and the celebration of radical anniversaries' (Belchem, 1990 p. 114). It has been claimed as the first working-class political party, and it certainly deserves at least as much attention as the Anti-Corn Law League in studies of extra-parliamentary political organization, especially given the difficult legal and financial circumstances under which it operated (its period of maximum growth overlapped with a particularly devastating trade depression). However we label it, it was an important and perhaps a path-breaking innovation. But it did not remain unchallenged as the central focus of the regrouped Chartist movement, and the conflicts which emerged from 1841 onwards tell us much about the persistently fissiparous nature of Chartism (Belchem, 1990 p. 111; Epstein, 1982 p. 220; Charlton, 1997 p. 28).

## New Directions

Three new directions in Chartism came to the fore in the spring of 1841: William Lovett's National Association for the Moral, Social and Political Improvement of the People; Henry Vincent's advocacy of 'Teetotal Chartism'; and the Birmingham Chartist Church which was established by Arthur O'Neill. Each of these initiatives had support from middle-class reformers, following in the wake of previous organizations such as the Leeds Parliamentary Reform Association of May 1840, which had sought to build an alliance between wealthy supporters of the Anti-Corn Law League and the sheer weight of numbers which the working class could bring to bear, only for its great rally of January 1841 to be taken over and subverted by the Chartists (Epstein, 1982 pp. 265–71). Each was denounced by O'Connor in the *Northern Star* in April 1841, when he attacked 'Church Chartism, Teetotal Chartism, Knowledge Chartism, and Household Suffrage Chartism', deploring the scope for division, diversion and dilution entailed by these initiatives and inviting local NCA groups to repudiate them. In practice, O'Neill's movement was of limited importance beyond Birmingham, where it formed part of a lasting controversy between rival Chartist groups over strategy and orientation. Similar initiatives were much stronger in Scotland, where they did not generate similar controversy. As with Vincent's teetotalism, O'Connor and other critics had no problem in accepting that such approaches could make a contribution to Chartism, and similar activities formed part of the NCA menu in many places; the polemic was driven by the company they kept, and here the higher profile of Lovett's so-called 'New Move' highlights the issues. A spell in prison, under health-sapping conditions, undermined the resolve of many of the most militant of the Chartists of 1839; and Lovett, who had been more assertive than he subsequently suggested, was no exception. With John Collins, who had shared his imprisonment in Warwick Gaol but was very much the junior partner in the enterprise, he published *Chartism, a New Organisation for the People* in October 1840, soon after his release. This contained political attacks on O'Connor and his allies for the violence and intolerance of their polemics, but its main concern was to advocate an educational programme to improve the knowledge, understanding and morality of the working classes, helping to further a climate of opinion in which the vote would be both achievable and responsibly used, and financed by popular subscription to keep the schools and colleges independent of the state and of middle-class philanthropy. If support for the first Chartist petition could be translated into penny-a-week subscriptions, a huge educational system under popular control could be constructed and sustained. To this end the formation of the National Association was proposed (Wiener, 1989 pp. 80–4). This was not necessarily divisive: it fitted into the broad spectrum of Chartist concerns, although it was noticeable that both Lovett and Collins themselves held aloof from the NCA on the grounds of its alleged illegality. What aroused O'Connor's wrath, and created a lasting rift, was the further publication in March 1841 of Lovett's *Address to the Political and Social Reformers*, which called for the establishment of the National Association as (in effect) a rival to the NCA, to bring about the educational and cultural regeneration which Lovett's *Chartism* pamphlet had advocated. This announced the arrival of the 'New Move', as Lovett secured 73 and later 87 signatures of leading Chartists in endorsement of his manifesto; but O'Connor and the *Northern Star* showed fierce hostility, especially when the scheme was supported by middle-class reform groups and (the kiss of death) by the Irish repealer and arch-opponent of

Chartism, Daniel O'Connell. The conflict conjured up raw recent memories of the splits in London Chartism and the London Working Men's Association with which Lovett had been associated in the movement's early days, and it did not help that Lovett had clearly been organizing in secret, envisaging an alternative and rival structure and orientation for the movement. O'Connor and his allies were able to drum up effective opposition, especially in the industrial heartlands of Lancashire and Yorkshire from which Lovett drew scant support. The 'New Move' was marginalized, although the National Association survived until 1849, after bitter and damaging conflict in which accusations of intimidation and dictation from the O'Connor party were difficult to discount; but it should be emphasized that those who rejected it were not opposed to temperance, or Christianity, or educational reform being associated with Chartism: what they feared was the dissipation of the movement's energies (and, no doubt, challenges to their own power) through a proliferation of rival organizations and distracting additional agenda. They also feared the intervention of middle-class reformers, with their own priorities, in the movement; and the subsequent episode of the Complete Suffrage Union (CSU) suggests that their worries were not unfounded (Wiener, 1989 pp. 84–90; Epstein, 1982 pp. 240–5; D. Thompson, 1984 pp. 259–60).

Joseph Sturge, a Quaker reformer from Birmingham with a track record of activism in (for example) the Birmingham Political Union, the anti-slavery movement and the campaign against a centralized police force, began his attempt to build a 'complete suffrage' movement in late 1841, pulling together outward-looking supporters of the Anti-Corn Law League who were frustrated by the narrowness of its concerns. In collaboration with the nonconformist minister Edward Miall, he sought to pursue 'full, fair and free representation' for 'the people' in parliament, and the movement gathered support especially among middle-class nonconformity, although as with similar earlier campaigns it lacked support in the northern industrial districts. This was an attempt to make radical reform look respectable, and it attracted the same group of Chartists as Lovett's 'New Move'; indeed, Lovett himself was an eager participant in the meetings of February and April 1842 at which middle-class and working-class representatives met to clarify the CSU's programme. Where Lovett and his allies would not budge, however, was in sticking to the Charter itself: no alternative definition of complete suffrage was acceptable, although the April conference postponed a definite decision on the status of the Charter until the autumn. Sturge's middle-class supporters wanted to shed the Charter, with its insurrectionary symbolism and association with fierce and threatening rhetoric; but those who had fought for it, Lovett included, and celebrated its history, would abandon neither the name nor the Six Points. The attitude of O'Connor and the *Northern Star* was ambivalent: the CSU was too closely associated with Free Trade and the Anti-Corn Law League to be acceptable, but eventually a strategy of infiltration rather than outright opposition was adopted. Chartists of all shades actively (indeed physically in the violence associated with the campaign) supported Sturge when he stood for the open and radical constituency of Nottingham at a by-election in the summer, and when the autumn conference of the CSU eventually took place in December 1842, after the Chartists had sought time to regroup following the wave of strikes and arrests in August and September, O'Connor himself and other representatives of the NCA stood in the elections to nominate delegates. They were successful enough (O'Connor being elected as one of the six delegates from Sturge's home territory of Birmingham) to stiffen the resistance to the proposed replacement of the Charter by a 96-clause Bill of Rights, as advocated by a section of the CSU, and eventually O'Connor and Lovett joined forces to insist that the Charter was the only basis for collaboration. This was just a tactical and temporary reconciliation, but it ensured that the CSU was kept at arm's length and allowed to wither: neither side would accept the other's conditions for joint action. O'Connor had entertained high hopes of winning over hard-pressed shopkeepers to the Charter during the turbulent summer of 1842, but his deployment of the language of class conflict, the rhetoric of 'unshorn chins and fustian jackets' and the continued attachment to a social policy, all kept mainstream middle-class radicalism at arm's length (Wiener, 1989 pp. 90–4; D. Thompson, 1984 pp. 262–70; Epstein, 1982 pp. 287–93; Ward, 1973 pp. 158–60, 165–6; Gammage, 1969 pp. 241–5).

The CSU initiative was partly a response to the modest but genuine success of the Chartist intervention in the General Election of 1841. Several Chartist candidates stood, but none came close to election; what impressed contemporaries, however, was the disciplined way in which Chartist voters were seen to act as a collectivity in support of the candidates recommended by their leaders. Where there was no Chartist candidate, voters were enjoined to support whoever was deemed the most radical, with support for democratic reform (as in the case of J.A. Roebuck at Bath) coming ahead even of opposition to the New Poor Law as a touchstone. Where no other differentiation could be made, votes were to go to Tories rather than Whigs. This was not, as (for example) J.T. Ward has suggested, the continuation of an affinity between O'Connorite Chartism and Tory radicalism, forged in the factory reform and anti-New Poor Law campaigns. Epstein argues that such an alliance was always illusory where the Charter itself was concerned, and that opposition to the Whigs was based on antipathy to their record and on the hope of undermining them as a party, leaving a gap which might be filled by a more radical party with some Chartist sympathies. This was not a universal perception: Bronterre O'Brien, for example, argued that where the choice lay between Whig and Tory the only principled course was abstention. Moreover, the new political alignment did not happen, but the Chartists' efforts to influence outcomes impressed contemporaries as making a material contribution to the Whigs' defeat, helping to create the frame of mind in which Sturge and his allies chose to reach out to suitable figures within the movement (Epstein, 1982 pp. 276–86; Ward, 1973 pp. 150–1, 156).

### The Second Petition and the 'General Strike' of 1842

More exciting developments awaited in 1842, when Chartism reached a second climax with the presentation of a second Petition for the Charter and the general strike which swept across the northern and midland industrial districts, and took tentative hold elsewhere, in late summer. No lasting gains were forthcoming, and the revolutionary undercurrents of 1839 were far less in evidence, but this was another high point in the movement's popularity, again coinciding with a severe trade depression. Chartism's resurgence as a mass movement perhaps began with the release of Feargus O'Connor from York Castle at the end of August 1841; as Epstein comments, 'He was honoured with one of the most elaborate demonstrations of popular support in the history of

English working-class radicalism.' This began a succession of 'mass demonstrations, triumphal processions and soirees' as O'Connor toured the country and signatures were gathered for the second great Petition (Epstein, 1982 p. 286). A new Convention was organized, this time elected by ballot, and met for three weeks in April 1842 to oversee the presentation of a document which went further than that of 1839, in that it demanded the repeal of the Poor Law Amendment Act and the Act of Union between Britain and Ireland, as well as attacking various economic abuses. This attachment of other demands to the Charter had been controversial in Scotland, but when the petition was presented at the beginning of May 1842 it was said to bear 3,317,752 signatures. This was an astounding achievement, which needs to be emphasized: there were more than twice as many signatories as in 1839. Chartism had more popular support than ever, and it was better-organized; but the petition was rejected much as before, attracting fewer than 50 votes in the Commons, and the movement again faced the problem of what to do when constitutional agitation failed, especially as there was general agreement that insurrection, or the threat of it, was no longer credible given the confidence of the State and the effectiveness of its repressive apparatus. Soon afterwards, a further wave of anger was generated by the death in captivity of an imprisoned Sheffield Chartist, Samuel Holberry, whose prison conditions clearly contributed to his death, and whose funeral attracted a demonstration of perhaps 50,000 people and a spate of speeches and commemorative verse (D. Thompson, 1984 pp. 280–1; Epstein, 1982 p. 294; Ward, 1973 pp. 156–7, 160–2).

It was at this high point of enthusiasm and frustration that the strike wave of the summer of 1842 broke and was (partially and temporarily) channelled into the Chartist cause. At the end of July the factory masters in Stalybridge and Ashton-under-Lyne, a few miles south-east of Manchester, decided to impose a further 25 per cent wage cut on a workforce which had already endured reductions and short-time working during the worst depression of the whole Chartist period. They encountered fierce resistance, and after a series of mass meetings (several thousand strong) the cotton workers of Ashton, Stalybridge, Hyde and Dukinfield agreed to strike, not only against the specific wage cuts but also for 'a fair day's wage for a fair day's work'. Some local meetings also carried motions to compel the advocates of Corn Law repeal to pay income tax, to obtain arms to defend the lives and property of the working class, and for the Charter to become the law of the land; and there was much discussion of the Charter itself. On 7 August speakers at a meeting on Mottram Moor, a favourite Chartist gathering-place, assured those present that a general strike for the Charter was planned for Lancashire and Cheshire, to start the next day; and the next morning the strikers went on a march to spread the stoppage to neighbouring towns and make it universal. Over the next two days the strike spread to Manchester and beyond, as the processions turned out workplace after workplace with systematic determination. By 15 August the strike embraced 'almost all the cotton workers of Lancashire, Cheshire and Yorkshire, and most miners from Staffordshire up to Lanarkshire' in western Scotland (Jenkins, 1980 p. 104). At its peak perhaps 500,000 workers were on strike, from Dundee to Cornwall, although Lancashire, Cheshire and West Yorkshire around Halifax remained the strongpoints. Most of the strikers had embraced the Charter as the goal of the strike, by voting for it at a mass meeting as the only way to safeguard any material gains which industrial action might achieve. The long-desired fusion between economic and political action and goals seemed to have been achieved (Jenkins, 1980 p. 104; Belchem, 1990 p. 119). In mid-August a series of trades conferences took place in Manchester and district, at which elected delegates confirmed their pursuit of the Charter by overwhelming votes. This was a completely novel set of developments which had unrolled with such speed as to take the authorities by surprise. Industry fell silent, and troops, police and magistrates were defied. Chelsea pensioners and special constables refused to act, or fled. Those Chartists who had hoped for an eruption from the grassroots of the angry and exploited, from which a revolution might be built, were full of hope and expectation, tinged with apprehension.

It was not to be: the power of the State was ultimately too strong, and the movement's national leadership, which was as startled as the authorities by the size, scope and speed of the movement's growth, drew back from 'waging war against recognized authority', despite the enthusiasm of the fiercely combative Peter Murray McDouall and the NCA executive to encourage the spread of the strike for the Charter and see what would happen (Epstein, 1982 p. 297). O'Connor and the *Northern Star* discountenanced the language of revolution, partly through fear of subsequent legal consequences, and spread the notion that the strike had been deliberately provoked by the Anti-Corn Law League to frighten the government into repeal; if so, they reaped the whirlwind. The authorities, national and local, were alarmed: Sir James Graham, the Home Secretary, thought the situation to be more dangerous than in 1839. Although the strike did not take hold to any extent in London, the troops who were sent north on the new railways had to run a gauntlet of angry protest from crowds who lined the streets from the barracks to Euston station. The authorities at first temporized with the strikers until they could regroup their forces but, when sufficient force was available, it was used to break up meetings (with bloodshed in some places, most infamously at Preston on 13 August, when four demonstrators were killed by the 72nd Highlanders), and to enforce the arrest of the movement's leaders. This took the momentum out of the strike, and by the end of August the demand for the Charter was fading as immediate wage-related issues returned to the fore. Gradually, groups of strikers returned to work in September; but it was not until the end of the month that the Manchester weavers went back, and in most cases the proposed wage cuts were withdrawn. Here and there, actual wage increases were achieved. The strike was an impressive achievement, though it never passed beyond a regional core of intense activity and never genuinely promised to achieve the Charter (Jenkins, 1980 pp. 161–218; Epstein, 1982 pp. 294–8; Belchem, 1990 pp. 118–19; D. Thompson, 1984 pp. 282–96).

The post-strike repression ranged widely. Leaders and activists were imprisoned with scant observance of legal niceties, and remanded for long periods with enormous sums demanded for bail. Perhaps 1,500 people were brought before the lower courts and special commissions: 200 were transported, some for life. At a more elevated level, the government planned a show trial for treasonable conspiracy, aiming to catch O'Connor and the trade union leaders in the same net. Significantly, it then retreated from this position, trying Feargus O'Connor and 58 others (including several members of the NCA executive) on the lesser charge of seditious conspiracy at Lancaster in March 1843, but the 31 people who were found guilty on one or two of the five counts in the indictment were released without sentence because of a mistake in drawing up the charges. We shall return to the issues raised by this retreat from severity in a later chapter (Epstein, 1982 pp. 300–1; Jenkins, 1980 pp. 219–39; Yeo, in Epstein and Thompson (eds), 1982 p. 366).

There is convincing evidence that the strike was well-organized, with well-defined targets and a clear agenda, especially in the Manchester area. Older forms of popular protest, like the pulling down of houses, were current in the Staffordshire Potteries, but in and around Manchester magistrates testified to the orderliness of the crowd, and most factory workers joined the strike voluntarily. The older emphasis on the strike as the 'Plug Plot', based on the emptying of factory boilers to enforce closures, tends to trivialize: this was a serious movement which was sustained for nearly two months in the face of severe economic hardship, and the political content of support for the Charter was there from the beginning. Many of the organizers were both trade union activists and Chartists; and where the strike was most 'political', it was also most orderly. This was, perhaps, the high water mark of active popular support for the Charter. After the summer of 1842, with the failure of the second Petition and the suppression of the strike, it was hard to see a plausible way forward for the movement, especially when the proffered alliance with the CSU was rejected.

## Retreat and Regrouping: the Land Plan and Other Initiatives

As in the aftermath of 1839, Chartism retreated into its shell; but this time the lull lasted longer. The local social life of the movement, through the National Charter Association's branches and other bodies, remained lively: indeed, it was boosted by the additional resources which an upturn in the economy made available to working people, even as they lost the urgency and militancy which accompanied industrial depression. More attention was paid to the debating societies, socials, co-operative trading initiatives and schools, and to sustaining the upkeep of meeting halls, in the absence of a big petitioning campaign to channel energies. The most important initiative of the mid-1840s was O'Connor's Land Plan, which helped to provide a sense of purpose and a set of attainable goals for Chartists during a difficult period. This initiative had long been foreshadowed in O'Connor's speeches, which had signalled the artificiality of industrial society, and the value of pushing wages up by enabling workers to move out of the labour market on to the land, thereby offering choices and a raised basic standard of living to all. Detailed proposals were flagged up in 1843, when O'Connor published a cheap part-work, *The management of small farms*, which expounded his ideas on labour-intensive husbandry. In 1845 the Chartist Land Company was established, to buy land which would then be distributed by lot to the shareholders, enabling them to set up as smallholders in what Epstein describes as 'an alternative political economy, one based upon independent production and small commodity exchange, limited ownership and competition' (Epstein, 1982 p. 313). This was particularly attractive to hand-loom weavers and similar hard-pressed craft workers, as samples from the lists of shareholders make clear; and it also gave a novel boost to Chartism's popularity in rural areas which had normally been stony ground. The Company was enormously popular: by August 1847 there were 43,847 shareholders, and as many again had joined by the end of the year, as the Chartist settlements proliferated. That the scheme was not successful in the long run owed something to the problems faced by industrial workers who tried to become smallholders, but more to the legal obstacles which were placed in the way of this kind of popular initiative by officials who placed the narrowest possible interpretations on the restrictive laws on obtaining legal recognition and protection. The Company had to be wound up in 1851, but it was neither eccentric nor irresponsible: indeed, it was part of a much wider strand of 'back to the land' thought in these years, and local branches of the Land Plan organization were often the seedbeds for Chartist revival in 1847–8 (D. Thompson, 1984 pp. 299–306; Yeo, in Epstein and Thompson (eds), 1982 pp. 366–70; Epstein, 1982 pp. 312–13; Ward, 1973 p. 179–83; Jones, 1975 pp. 128–37; Belchem, 1990 pp. 121–3).

While this was happening O'Connor and the NCA were coming round to acceptance of piecemeal reform, both on the factory issue and the Corn Laws, and Chartist candidates were doing well in the 1847 General Election, where O'Connor actually managed to win a seat in the unusually open constituency of Nottingham. Chartists were also making headway in local government, where the franchise was less exclusive, and they were particularly effective in Leeds. But by late 1847 there were signs of a revival at national level, and 1848, the 'year of revolutions' across Europe,

31

was to see the last great petitioning campaign and the final confrontation with the forces of authority on the national stage (D. Thompson, 1984 p. 309; Ward, 1973 p. 175).

## 1848: the Last Climax

The revival of Chartism pre-dated the French Revolution of February 1848. It was given added strength by new links with Irish campaigners for the repeal of the Act of Union between Britain and Ireland, which brought new recruits to Chartism in places with substantial Irish populations in England, especially Liverpool and London, as well as in Ireland itself. These new links were eased by the death of Daniel O'Connell, the nationalist leader whose acceptance of the New Poor Law and all that went with it had been anathema to the Chartists, and by angry Irish reaction to the Great Famine, which reached its grim peak in 1847. Chartism had also recruited a new generation of English activists, from Ernest Jones and G.W.M. Reynolds to a large number of local organizers, and their radicalism was all the more outspoken for not having been through the dangers and traumas of 1839 and 1842. The third Petition aimed at a record five million signatories, and a Convention was convened in London on 4 April to watch over its presentation on 10 April. This was to be prefaced by a huge meeting on Kennington Common, south of the Thames, from which a tremendous procession was to accompany the Petition to Westminster, and (many hoped) to inaugurate the revolution (D. Thompson, 1984 pp. 307–19; Saville, 1987 pp. 80–101; Belchem, 1990 pp. 127–31).

The authorities were concerned, but confident. The February revolution in France, and subsequent stirrings elsewhere, had galvanized English radicals into sharpening pikes, making bullets and preparing for glory; but reports of its excesses, and of the socialistic doctrines which were said to prevail, polarized opinion and encouraged all who thought they had something to lose (including many working people) to rally to the ancient constitution, which was presented as being in danger from untried abstract foreign doctrines which also threatened property. Turbulent meetings and riots in London, Glasgow and elsewhere during March allowed the authorities to oil their repressive machinery, which had been greatly reinforced (in number of police and soldiers, and credibility of special constables) during the 1840s, and aided by the spread of railways and the telegraph system. The apocalyptic language of some speakers at the

32

Convention, assiduously reported in the press, also alienated people who might have been sympathetic or neutral. In the event, the Kennington meeting was so effectively policed that it posed no practical threat to authority, although the Queen had been dispatched to her Isle of Wight residence as a precaution. Some may have stayed away because of the fear of violence, others because their leaders had proscribed it; and the petition had to be taken to parliament by a deputation in a cab. On arrival it was laughed out of court, on the alleged grounds that two-thirds of the signatures were obviously fraudulent, some risibly so, including that of the arch-Tory MP Colonel Sibthorpe. The petition was withdrawn, and the great day sputtered out in confusion (Saville, 1987 pp. 102–29).

This was not the end, although textbooks following the propaganda of Victorian historians have often presented it as such. Obviously a movement of this strength, channelling such emotional energy and commitment, could not disappear overnight. The National Assembly, which had been organized with high hopes of becoming an alternative parliament, met in May 1848 in London, but its deliberations were dominated by empty rhetoric and division; more important were the grass-roots initiatives which developed in May and June. Support for organized Chartism continued to grow in London during these months, and it was here especially that meetings and marches on Clerkenwell Green and Bonner's Fields, and on one provocative occasion through the West End shopping districts, kept the authorities on the alert. Plans for insurrection were clearly being made behind closed doors, although much of the evidence is suspect; and in Liverpool, Bradford and the cotton districts around Manchester there were similar developments. Surveillance and the fear of spies made it difficult to co-ordinate such activities, although there was much talk of using carrier pigeons (turning a popular working-class hobby to political account); and this aspect of the movement was not suppressed until the arrest of large numbers of the leadership, local and national, during the summer. The authorities also became much more confident in banning meetings and suppressing demonstrations, with occasional outbreaks of police violence. This last phase of insurrectionary Chartism, combined with events in Ireland, demonstrates that the failure of 10 April 1848 was not the demoralizing fiasco that the mainstream media sought to claim (Saville, 1987 Chapter 5; Goodway, 1982).

## Decline and Transformation

But this was the beginning of the end for Chartism as an organized political movement. The revival of 1848 was limited in geographical scope: of 1,009 places where Dorothy Thompson found evidence of Chartist organization between 1839 and 1848, only 207 were active in the latter year, 42 of which had emerged since 1845. Moreover, the 1848 campaign took place alongside an impressive expansion in petitioning for more limited measures of parliamentary reform, which must have recruited many former Chartists (Miles Taylor, 1995 pp. 104–5). O'Connor himself retreated from earlier strategies, developing ideas about a closer relationship with organized labour; and there was general acceptance of the futility of trying to intimidate or coerce an increasingly confident and widely supported central government. Ernest Jones, the confidant of Marx and Engels, captured the National Charter Association for his socialist policies after 1850, while others among the leadership decided that the only way forward was to collaborate with middle-class reformers for whatever piecemeal concessions could be obtained. In some provincial centres Chartism had an extended afterlife: it was still possible for meetings in the Manchester area to attract crowds several hundred strong in the mid-1850s, and Chartist rhetoric was deployed, for example, in the great Preston strike and lock-out of 1853–4. Halifax, which Jones made his base during the 1850s, sustained a strong Chartist presence into mid-decade; Jones won the show of hands there at the hustings for the General Election as late as 1852, although only 38 of the official electorate would vote for him. Chartist supporters survived to feed their ideas and commitment into the reform movements of the mid-1860s which helped to promote the Second Reform Act. The decline of Chartism was a slow, tangled affair, as splinter-groups proliferated; the reasons for it are explored in later chapters. Meanwhile, after this initial account of the movement's trajectory between the late 1830s and the mid-1850s, we move on to examine the roots of Chartism's support, and the complex mixture of motivations which lay behind the patterns of its distribution by region, place and time (Kirk, 1985 pp. 67–70; Tiller, in Epstein and Thompson (eds), 1982 pp. 311–44; Dutton and King, 1981).

# 2
# Chartist Goals

## Chartism and Practical Reform

The core of Chartist aspiration was expressed in the Six Points, and the Charter's distinctive version of parliamentary reform was what pulled the movement together. It represented a tradition of agitation which spanned two generations and laid claim to myths and martyrs, none more powerful than those which surrounded the Peterloo Massacre of 1819. Some of the most important languages of Chartism were those which gave pride of place to political principle, whether they based the entitlement to manhood suffrage on natural rights drawn from first principles or on the lost legacy of the free-born Englishman. One of the central concerns of the movement was the conquest of citizenship. The Complete Suffrage movement and other compromises and diversions of the early 1840s, such as William Lovett's schooling-focused National Association for the Moral, Social and Political Improvement of the People, weakened Chartism at its roots because they drew support and energy away from the central authority and integrity of the Six Points. Chartism's essential nature was political. But much of its support was drawn from people who had practical grievances, and whose living standards were threatened by specific aspects of government legislation and the working of the legal system. These people were drawn into Chartism because its political proposals promised a legislature which might redress their grievances, restore lost rights and create a fairer legislative framework for trade union activities; these were working-class issues. Chartism had a few principled supporters among the substantial middle classes, and a considerable following among small traders and fringe professional people, many of whom were former manual workers who had been blacklisted for their trade union and radical political activity; but it was overwhelmingly a working-class movement in its social composition: a movement whose backbone and numerical predominance was drawn from wage-earning manual workers. Under these circumstances the agenda of Chartism beyond the Charter was crucial to the movement's popularity, although the aims of some reformers within the movement were not always congruent with or even sympathetic towards those of others. Sources of strength in one context might be fomenters of discord in another. But the pursuit of this question takes us beyond the more abstract questions of the language(s) of Chartism to look at the decidedly practical goals which helped to attach people to the movement; and the local case-studies which are necessary to understand the differing soils in which Chartism took root again take us into a deeper realm of explanation than the linguistic analysis of the Chartist press, or even Chartist autobiographies, ever can.

What is clear, at the outset, is that simplistic explanations which regard Chartism as solely a 'bread and butter' or 'knife and fork' question, and even as almost a knee-jerk or reflex response to economic adversity, a disorder born out of frustration on the part of the rash, uneducated, impatient and starving, carry little conviction. The phrases in question were current among Chartists themselves to justify the fierce idioms they sometimes used and to stiffen the conviction and resolve of their hearers, but Chartists had principles and aspirations which such condescending interpretations from outside their culture signally fail to recognize. It is true that the movement generated its most numerous following in times of economic hardship, in the trade depressions of 1839 and 1842; and root and branch measures were more likely to have a widespread appeal at times when the existing system appeared to be breaking down, as in these apocalyptic times. But we shall see that the map of Chartist support did not coincide with the areas or trades which experienced the deepest poverty or the most endemic, day-by-day insecurity, whether among agricultural day-labourers, or in the unpredictable setting of the docks and seaports, or the sweated and seasonal trades of London's East End. There was much more to Chartism than the politics of hunger: there was political conviction and a measured anger at specific injustices which had been devised and nourished by successive parliaments, especially (and with desperate irony) in the aftermath of Reform. Indeed, Chartism can be differentiated from earlier movements for radical political reform in that its genesis came in the bitter ashes of the apparent victory of 1832 which proved merely to have opened the door to a more sustained and concerted attack on working-class ways of life and institutions than had hitherto been experienced, as the advocates of *laissez-faire*, 'philosophic radicalism' and Malthusian explanations of poverty (which blamed over-population arising from improvident marriages and unrestrained fecundity) were given their heads in the new parliament.

## The New Poor Law

Perhaps the most important set of grievances which arose from the legislative work of the post-Reform Whig governments to feed mass support for Chartism came from the implementation of the New Poor Law of 1834. This was a particularly potent symbol of the failure of the 1832 Reform Act to live up to the hopes that many had entertained during the reform campaigns. Indeed, it confirmed the worst suspicions of those radicals who regarded it from the outset as making the world safe for the propertied classes. The post-Reform parliaments of the mid-1830s seemed to have made life even more insecure for working people who had campaigned for a more radical measure and had been obliged to accept a compromise. The threat of the workhouse, with the expectation that it would break up families, impose starvation wages and treat paupers more severely than criminals (especially in conjunction with the Anatomy Act of 1832 (Ruth Richardson, 1988), which made unclaimed pauper corpses available for medical dissection), lay at the core of popular assumptions that recipients of poor relief would be humiliated and degraded even when their poverty was no fault of their own. Campaigners against the New Poor Law, which was being introduced into the industrial districts of Lancashire and the West Riding of Yorkshire in 1837, were readily drawn into the broader campaigns of the Chartists, seeing no redress through a political system which was

37

visibly dominated by enthusiastic proponents of a particularly hard-nosed economic orthodoxy of *laissez-faire*, especially where welfare and labour markets were concerned. The campaign against the New Poor Law was a potent recruiter of Chartists in the textile-manufacturing districts of the Lancashire and Yorkshire Pennines, where the movement was to be particularly strong and enduring. This was, in context, a logical and even seamless progression. The Poor Law issue was especially instrumental in drawing women into active support for Chartism, with its imposition of full responsibility for illegitimate children on to the mother, unless she was able to prove the father's identity in court, and (much more importantly) its explicit threat to break up families in every trade depression or other crisis, which bore particularly heavily on women's roles and priorities (Schwarzkopf, 1991; D. Thompson, 1984 pp. 34–5, 120–51). Some of the fiercest and most effective Chartist rhetoric against the inhumanity of dominant ideas within the reformed political system was stimulated and informed by the New Poor Law and the language of its proponents, whose assumptions about working-class idleness, profligacy and thriftlessness provided obvious targets for impassioned but well-founded denunciation.

### Trade Union and Workplace Grievances

Another boost for Chartist support in the textile areas came from the long-lasting grievances of the hand-loom weavers, who were threatened with the workhouse in trade depression and old age because of the long-term fall in piece-rate wages which left them working ever-longer hours to sustain the most basic of living standards, and left some of them dependent on wages supplements from the Poor Law which were threatened by the new orthodoxy of denying relief outside the workhouse. The fact that this turned out to be impracticable and unenforceable in practice did not diminish the threat it posed to vulnerable people in the late 1830s and early 1840s. The weavers, whose numbers in the Lancashire cotton industry were reviving sharply in the boom of the mid-1830s and whose decline came later than is often assumed (there were still between 40,000 and 77,000 in the county in 1851) (Timmins, 1993 pp. 92–7, 110), had been campaigning for more than a generation for the restoration of minimum wages, and for restrictions on apprenticeship which were supposed to limit labour supply and sustain wage-levels, but which had been repealed in 1814 by a parliament already increasingly in thrall to the doctrines of the free market. They had a long tradition of radical political activity, and hoped for great things from the reformed parliament, only to have their expectations dashed when a favourable Royal Commission report was countermanded by a second enquiry, packed by opponents of their cause, which dismissed their claims with contempt (Paul Richards, 1979). Here again, the outcome of 1832 was beginning to look like betrayal within a disturbingly short time.

More generally, trade unionists were increasingly disaffected by the failure of the reformed parliament to protect their interests against employers who were going on the offensive in the increasingly frequent and severe downturns of the trade cycle. The Combination Acts of 1799 might have had some of their teeth drawn in the mid-1820s, but there was still plenty of scope for prosecuting unionists for conspiracy and swearing illegal oaths, and strikers for leaving work without notice, and the dice continued to be visibly loaded in favour of the employers. The transportation in 1834 of the Tolpuddle Martyrs (Dorsetshire agricultural labourers who tried to form a union and were severely punished for swearing illegal oaths) brought an angry campaigning reaction from trade unions and their allies. Three years later in 1837, the judicial repression of the Glasgow cotton spinners' strike, when the leading officials of the union were tried for their lives for alleged conspiracy to murder a strike-breaker, and were transported for organizing illegal activities even though they were acquitted on the main charge, stimulated nationwide organization in support of the defendants and helped to pull trade unionists into political campaigns (D. Thompson, 1984 pp. 21–3).

As befits the evidence for the political dimensions to trade union concerns, but contrary to some older interpretations, it is now clear that trade unions were actively involved in Chartist activities: many branches, as well as individual members, saw legislative intervention as the only way to level the playing field between masters and workers, and understood the Charter to be the only way of bringing this about (Musson, 1976; Sykes, in Epstein and Thompson (eds), 1982). The hard evidence for this is strongest in the cotton-spinning district around Manchester, where craft unions joined factory workers in showing sustained and organized support for the Charter, which reached a climax at the 1842 general strike; but similar links were in evidence elsewhere and many individual trade unionists must have been drawn into Chartism because of the fairer legislative framework which the Charter seemed likely to make possible (Fyson and Sykes, in Epstein and Thompson (eds), 1982; Jenkins, 1980).

## Factory Reform and the Working-class Family

The Charter also offered better prospects for the fuller and more effective measure of factory reform which many contemporaries were urging. Campaigners argued that women's labour was being exploited to the detriment of the emergent ideal of the male breadwinner wage, thereby undermining masculine authority in the working-class home and threatening the family as an essential basis for social stability (Clark, 1992; Seccombe, 1993; Humphries and Horrell, 1995). Women and children, who (unlike men) were seen as incapable of bargaining on their own account in the labour market, were being forced into working hours and conditions which promoted deformity, disease and immorality, and which were likened by some to slavery. The Factory Act of 1833, with its restricted and contested definition of childhood, failure to reduce the working hours of adults and paucity of inspectors, did not satisfy the reformers' demands. Consequently, a sustained agitation for a ten-hour working day and further limitations on child labour was gathering in intensity just as the Chartist movement was germinating, fuelled by an attempt by principled advocates of the free market to exempt twelve-year-olds from the Act's restrictions on working hours in 1836. Too much should not be made of this: the most articulate advocates of factory reform were Tory paternalists whose motives were political as well as humanitarian, and who had no sympathy with the Chartist cause, while many working people were concerned to maximize family incomes, even at the cost of long working hours and illness, and objected to attempts to limit their options through paternalist legislation. On the other hand, some historians emphasize the self-interested aspects of the reform campaign within the factory workforce, arguing that the pursuit of the 'breadwinner' wage was aimed at winning men a privileged position in the labour market and defending it from the competition of women and children. This was a complex issue, and the links with Chartism were less clear-cut than in the

40

other cases. Nevertheless, it helped to expand and deepen Chartist support in the movement's strongholds in the factory districts of Lancashire and Yorkshire, not least by providing an additional demonstration of the ways in which parliamentary proceedings affected intimate aspects of the daily lives and family economics of working-class people who were excluded from the vote.

## The Social Origins of Chartist Activists

Some indication of the social structure of active Chartist support comes from an analysis of nominations to the General Council of the National Charter Association in 1841. Craftsmen employed at home or in small workshops on piece-rate wages were the most conspicuous group among a sample of 853, with 130 weavers, 97 shoemakers (a traditional radical occupation), 58 tailors, and 33 framework-knitters in the stocking trade. These occupations, and others like them, were under particular pressure from a system of competitive undercutting whereby the middlemen who put out the work set people against each other to bid down wages to the lowest level: this was a much more pervasive, though less conspicuous, problem than those associated with the factory system. Other craftsmen, such as carpenters and joiners, in 'the humbler skilled trades', under threat from machinery and the opening out of their occupations to competition as apprenticeship became harder to defend against the intrusion of untrained workers, were also prominent: they had a particular interest in sustaining their trade unions to protect what they saw as their property in acquired skills. Factory workers were also in evidence, and so were miners, but their regional concentration diluted their importance in a national sample. At this level of conspicuous activism, of people aspiring to involvement at national level, Chartism was clearly dominated by skilled craftsmen and outworkers in the textile and clothing trades (David Jones, 1975 pp. 30–2; Mather, 1980 pp. 17–20).

This social composition helps to explain why Chartists might be recruited through a perceived need for a measure of parliamentary reform which would bring about increased government intervention in the form of protective legislation, and expand the positive role of the state in poor relief. Chartist priorities in this regard, indeed, harked back to a 'moral economy' which placed traditional entitlements to fair prices, assistance in time of crisis, and the protection of property in the form of skills validated through apprenticeship, above the free play of market forces in the scale of proper government concerns, whether at local level or national. But Chartists might also be keen on dismantling expensive government machinery and removing restraints on trade when they thought they might benefit thereby; and the political certainties of the movement were accompanied by economic principles which sometimes looked contradictory, although the aim to improve the living standards and personal security of the politically excluded was entirely consistent.

## Chartism and the Repeal of the Corn Laws

The most tempting Free Trade measure among the sort of skilled craft workers, factory hands and small traders who were most likely to be drawn to Chartism was the repeal of the Corn Laws, which artificially inflated the price of bread to the apparent enrichment of a landed interest of aristocrats, gentry and prosperous farmers, and at the expense of industry. But repeal, which had its own high-profile campaign from 1838 onwards in the hands of the Anti-Corn Law League, was in practice a distraction from the Charter. It might seem probable that a parliament elected under the Six Points would remove the 'bread tax' as a high priority; but the League's middle-class leadership, based in Manchester and dominated by the manufacturing interest, presented repeal as a single-issue campaign, independent of the Charter. They encouraged the belief that it would be a panacea for all the ills of the working classes, improving the competitive position of British industry, boosting home demand for manufactured goods, encouraging potential competitors to concentrate on growing food for British markets rather than industrializing on their own account, and offering more regular work as well as cheaper food. When League spokesmen were unwise enough to draw attention to the possibility of reducing wages in line with cheaper food prices, however, they confirmed the worst suspicions of many Chartist leaders. Corn Law repeal was presented as desirable but not sufficient, and Chartists in the League's Manchester heartland emphasized that it was only acceptable as part of a broader package of reforms, including restrictions on the further spread of machinery, which could only be securely implemented by a parliament based on manhood suffrage: a programme which was anathema to the prosperous free-trading merchants and manufacturers who headed and funded the League. Chartists emphasized that legislative concessions on specific issues in an unreformed parliament were not sufficient: they were vulnerable to reversal at the first opportunity, whenever pressure from without was relaxed, and this applied to the Corn Law repeal as much as to the other contentious issues. The League's attempt to recruit working-class support in Manchester foundered on the rock of the general disposition of activists to put the Charter first and distrust the overtures of the large employers, and only when some of the local Irish were persuaded that the Chartists were traducing their national icon Daniel O'Connell did they intervene against them on the League's behalf on a few well-publicized occasions during 1841–2. Otherwise, Chartists were able to disrupt the League's mass meetings and take them over to pass resolutions in support of the Charter (Pickering, 1995 pp. 86–104). The campaigns proceeded side by side, but with no sustained positive contact or common action between them; and when the Corn Laws were actually repealed in 1846 it made little direct difference to the trajectory of Chartism itself, which had passed its peak by that time but proved capable of a resurgence in 1848 which, as described in Chapter 1, thoroughly frightened the authorities.

### Chartists and Government

More prominent as a Chartist characteristic was distrust of big and expensive government, except when it intervened to protect workers' living standards and organizations. This applied both at national and local level, and was impelled by the movement's inherited critique of the corruption of the old constitution in church and state. This was readily extendable to all imaginable forms of government, including those which were dominated by the new capitalist middle class, who were seen as just as oppressive and potentially corrupt as the old aristocracy and its allies. When Chartists won seats on local government bodies, as in Manchester and Salford (following up an established local radical tradition of municipal activism), in Leeds and in the Staffordshire Potteries, they tended to oppose innovations which concentrated power (and especially policing) in local middle-class hands, but also attacked centralizing tendencies in national government and resisted increased local government expenditure. They preferred to work through those existing structures of government to which they had a measure of access, and it was from perspectives like these that Manchester's Chartists opposed the incorporation of the town as a borough in 1838, which would (they argued) concentrate additional power in the hands of the large employers (Pickering, 1995 pp. 73–85; Gatrell, 1982; Fyson, in Epstein and Thompson (eds), 1982; J.F.C. Harrison, in Briggs, 1959). Chartism in general favoured voluntary organizations and self-help rather than what would later be called state socialism, and it is significant that (for example) there was no working-class movement for public health reform.

Above all, Chartists were suspicious of the coercive arm of government; and with good reason, as the marshalling of armed forces and the building of barracks in disaffected areas to overawe potential insurrectionaries and repress protest were to demonstrate. The new police forces with their military-style ethos and disciplinary aspirations, which were proliferating under the Municipal Corporations Act of 1835 and the act of 1839 which encouraged the setting up of county constabularies, were regarded with grave suspicion by Chartists who feared the vesting of repressive powers in forces controlled by the local magistracy, which might engender (as was suggested in Manchester) a 'tyranny of the bloated rich' (Gatrell, 1982). The implications of the Irish Coercion Act of 1833, especially if its provisions were translated to other parts of the United Kingdom, also generated fears of the abuse of executive power which helped to stimulate attachment to Chartism. The Act empowered Lords Lieutenant in Ireland to suppress and criminalize any meeting they might deem dangerous to public safety, and if one of these functionaries labelled his county 'disturbed' there were even stricter restrictions on public meetings, with the introduction of curfews and military justice. The fear of such draconian measures being extended to England both boosted and overshadowed Chartism in the years that followed (D. Thompson, 1984 pp. 18–19).

More generally, the Irish dimension to Chartist recruitment should not be neglected. Here again, opposition to the power of the British state was at issue, and when the campaign for the repeal of the Act of Union between Britain and Ireland gathered momentum in 1848 it drew large numbers of Irish immigrants into endorsing the Charter in the hope that a purified parliament would enact the desired reforms. The trials of three Irish activists under draconian new legislation gave a further boost to this campaign (D. Thompson, 1984 pp. 326–9; Saville, 1987 p. 76). But there was already much Irish activity under the Chartist umbrella. Chartism inherited an earlier radical tradition of concern for Irish abuses, and Feargus O'Connor's formal linking of Irish Repeal with the Charter in October 1841 acknowledged the aspirations of Irish supporters of the Charter from its earliest days (Pickering, 1995 pp. 95–6). The commitment of the Irish working-class community to Chartism is impossible to measure with any precision, but wherever local studies probe below the surface evidence of Irish involvement in grass-roots leadership emerges.

To return to the question of Chartist suspicion of 'big government', it should be noted that Chartist support for the logic of free trade covered a range of themes from abolition of the 'taxes on knowledge' (newspaper stamp and paper duties) to the dismantling of the privileged legal and constitutional positions of the Church of England (especially its powers to tax for the upkeep of clergy and church property which were coming under increasingly effective attack in urban industrial settings), and (through institutions such as the law of entail, which preserved aristocratic estates from the corrosive logic of market forces) the aristocracy. Dorothy Thompson goes so far as to bracket the first of these issues with the New Poor Law as the two most important aspects of the programmes of the post-Reform governments in generating popular reactions which fed directly into Chartism, especially when the Newspaper Act of 1836 outraged popular opinion by reducing the stamp to one penny but failing to abolish (D. Thompson, 1984 pp. 29, 40–1; Wiener, 1969; Hollis, 1970). By conventional standards, the movement seems not to have had a consistent set of economic ideas: it sought protective government interference in prices and labour markets where this seemed to safeguard working people's living standards, while endorsing the logic of free trade where it suited Chartist goals, as in religion, the book and newspaper trades and the shrinking of 'big government', especially in its coercive policing and military roles. In Liverpool, for example, Chartism's early growth was stunted by its lack of a purchase or position on the debate between protection and free trade in international markets, which was more important than the franchise issue to many waterfront workers, whose livelihoods depended on such questions and a large proportion of whom could already vote as freemen of the borough in this unusual constituency (Moore, in Belchem (ed.), 1992).

## Chartism and 'Moral Economy'

On its own terms, however, Chartism's position can be given coherence under a 'moral economy' label, as articulated by E.P. Thompson in his *Customs in common* in an eighteenth-century setting (Thompson, 1990). Chartists believed that old rights of access to and use of land, together with government intervention to protect living standards by preventing prices and wages from fluctuating beyond a traditionally acceptable range, should be maintained. They sought to protect themselves from the threatening influences of a 'free market' in industrial labour, whose dice were loaded in favour of employers and the propertied: a set of beliefs which was heretical in the eyes of the ruling classes of the 1830s and 1840s. At the same time they wanted to protect and extend freedoms in the realm of ideas (including the freedom to challenge orthodox political economy) and self-expression: an area in which free trade seemed not to be such a self-evident good in the eyes of authority. An aspiration to independence, to the right to the unmolested and inoffensive pursuit of subsistence, lay behind a range of concerns within Chartism, from Lovett's proposals for an alternative system of popular schooling financed by subscriptions from the signatories to the 1839 petition, to the Land Plan itself, which offered the prospect of a return to a kind of 'dual economy' combining small-scale agriculture and domestic manufacture, promising a measure of autonomy to small producers. This system was well remembered and, in some areas, still far from extinct. These were, in principle, modest aspirations, but the economic changes and dominant systems of thought at the time made them difficult to attain and pulled them into the contentious arena of radical politics.

## Chartist Strongholds

As befitted the pattern of fears and hopes which generated support for the Charter in pursuit of other goals, Chartism was strongest in those industrial areas where the cyclical trade depressions of the late 1830s and 1840s, coupled with the dependence of families in declining handicraft trades on outdoor relief, made the New Poor Law seem especially threatening, while community ties and mutual assistance societies such as trade unions and friendly societies (which insured their members against sickness, injury and other contingencies) were particularly strong, enabling Chartism to colonize a popular associational culture. The threat to the trade unions themselves, which were increasingly beleagured in these years, gave added impetus to Chartist organization here; and these tended also to be the areas where a tradition of attachment to radical reform had roots which went back two generations to the 1790s. Belchem specifies as follows:

> The real Chartist strongholds ... were not the cities but the surrounding towns and out-townships, the typical industrial communities of the manufacturing districts – the textile towns of Lancashire, Cheshire and the West Riding (of Yorkshire); the hosiery, lace and glove-making areas of the east midlands; the depressed linen-weaving centres of Barnsley and Dundee; and the 'industrial villages' of the mining and ironworking districts, the north-east coalfield, the South Wales valleys and the Black Country. Here occupational ties were reinforced by other loyalties, by networks of mutual knowledge and trust which facilitated powerful and effective political organization.
>
> (Belchem, 1990 p. 105)

He might have added some reference to similar places in the Scottish Lowlands and around Carlisle; but this is generally a convincing picture.

The most impressive Chartist bulwarks were in the Pennine industrial areas of south-east Lancashire and the West Riding of Yorkshire, which combined factory industry with declining textile crafts and strong trade union and radical political traditions. The distribution of Chartist strength in the north-western counties of Lancashire, Cumberland and Westmorland (using the pre-1974 boundaries) provides a model with wider application. If we take the geographical distribution of signatories to the first great Chartist petition of 1839 as a rough indication of the movement's areas of strength and weakness, at least in the early years, we find that the highly specialized, rapidly growing cotton-spinning towns and industrial villages around Manchester showed the highest proportions of signatures to population, varying from one in three to one in eight or nine. We must bear in mind that it is impossible to match up local government or census districts with the areas which were given the same labels for the petition, and this means that the figures provide orders of magnitude without any pretensions to precision. This helps to explain why, on the count presented by Dorothy Thompson, Todmorden's Chartist petitioners added up to more than 100 per cent of the total population: we must not assume the presence of fraud on the scale which was used to discredit the petition of 1848, and similar phenomena are visible elsewhere, most spectacularly in Northampton (where the characteristic affinity between shoemakers and radical politics, so strongly emphasized by Dorothy Thompson, was obviously at work). Within the north-west itself, the positive correlation between developing 'cotton towns' and Chartism was strong, and it extended beyond the immediate Manchester region to embrace outposts of the cotton industry at Carlisle (where impoverished hand-loom weavers with a long radical political pedigree gave particular momentum to the movement), and other textile centres at Kendal (where middle-class support gave Chartism an unusually moderate temper) and Wigton (a market town with a linen-weaving tradition). Manchester itself was much less of a Chartist stronghold on this evidence, with signatories accounting for fewer than one in 30 of the population; but there was evidence of a much higher level of activity three years later. Recent research suggests that the town was more a centre both of Chartism and of factory industry than had been supposed in the 1970s and 1980s by historians who tended to emphasize the economic role of commerce rather than manufacture, the fragmentation of community and the difficulty of sustaining working-class organization in the cotton metropolis. Manchester's profile was certainly raised by the radicals of its industrial hinterland, for whom it was the obvious centre for mass meetings and demonstrations; but Pickering's work shows that it was also a strong Chartist centre on its own account. The north-west's other regional metropolis, Liverpool, lacked these militant surroundings, and (with other seaports which featured casual and sweated labour) it did not appear to be a major Chartist base, although one in fourteen of the population featured on the 1839 petition. The mining and heavy industry district of south-west Lancashire proved inhospitable to Chartism, just as it lacked the developed self-help and mutual aid traditions which were expressed through trade unions and friendly societies in the north-west's Chartist strongholds. Further north, the coal-mining areas of West Cumberland saw practically no Chartist activity, as the great landed estates which dominated these industrial areas and their seaport towns were able to freeze out all kinds of radical politics and trade unionism. As in most of Britain, too, the market towns and rural areas were infertile soil for the Chartist message, with only a token showing. It was generally difficult to export Chartism from the industrial and commercial centres into the agricultural districts, as the better-documented rural experience of (for example) Suffolk, Somerset and Wiltshire shows (Fearn and Pugh, in Briggs, (ed.), 1959). Wherever there was any hint of agricultural labourers being mobilized by and alongside industrial workers, as happened briefly around Saxmundham in Suffolk in late 1838 and early 1839 and at Crockerton Green near Warminster in February 1839, the county magistrates were particularly likely to write alarmist memoranda seeking help from the Home Office. But such phenomena were evanescent and ephemeral everywhere.

Two points should be made about the evidence on the distribution of Chartist strength within the economically diverse north-west of England, which contained the first industrial district to combine rapid urbanization with the rise of full-fledged factory industry: classic territory for a 'making of the working class', as many contemporary observers were only too aware, although not necessarily the artisan version celebrated by Edward Thompson in his famous book *The Making of the English Working Class*. First, different parts of the region 'peaked' at different times. Cotton towns such as Oldham and Preston, and their satellite industrial villages, were particularly active in the early years of the movement, showing an especially marked decline after the repression which followed the end of the great strike of August and September 1842, and failing to revive in the trade depression of 1846–7 or in the last great upsurge of the internationally revolutionary year of 1848. Reasons for this may be sought partly in the demoralizing impact of the repression itself, partly in the declining importance of the hand-loom weavers who played such a strong role in the movement's inception here. Second, we should emphasize the receding threat of the New Poor Law, in an area where it seemed especially disturbing on paper but its strictest provisions were not carried out in practice, coupled with the emergence of a less aggressive stance towards trade unions and other concessions by local elites on such issues as factory reform in the mid-1840s. Liverpool, on the other hand, saw its local Chartist movement peak in 1848, in response to the importance of the Irish issue in a setting where passions were heightened by the arrival of large numbers of destitute and disease-ridden refugees from the Irish potato famine. A survey of Chartist strongpoints and weaknesses towards the end of the 1840s would thus produce a rather different picture from the one based on the signatures attached to the 1839 petition; and it was in 1848 that Chartism in London reached its belated peak, continuing to gather momentum (with strong Irish support) for some weeks after the ill-fated Kennington demonstration of 10 April, while Bradford and Halifax (for example) similarly continued to alarm the authorities with well-supported demonstrations and fierce rhetoric.

### Class Consciousness?

The north-western evidence also draws attention to the question of how far, and under what conditions, Chartism should be regarded as a class-conscious working-class movement. This Marxist angle of vision highlights the drawing together of wage-labourers under the Chartist umbrella, conscious of their shared interests and injustices in opposition to the employers who took an unfair share of the fruits of their labours, and to the landowners whose revenues came from the unjust possession of broad acres which enabled them to manipulate the machinery of state to the disadvantage and exclusion of the people at large. Chartism, on this showing, provided a rhetoric and an understanding which could pull working people together across the boundaries of trade and workplace hierarchy which normally divided them, enabling them to rise up in pursuit of their common interests and entitlements as workers against a corrupt system, not only in trade union campaigns but in an assault on the whole paraphernalia of ruling-class power and institutions. The strongest statement of this position for a particular locality was Foster's book on Oldham, which argued that such a consciousness of class interests and identity passed beyond being the preserve of a committed and convinced minority of agitators in the 1830s and 1840s, and spread among the wage-earning people at large, to issue forth in the first instance in a great industrial dispute in 1834 which pulled workers together across a range of trades, and entailed a local political campaign to rescue the arrested and take control of the town's police force. But this politicization of the workers was to find its highest expression in the great strike of August and September 1842, when campaigners against wage reductions in a severe trade depression voted not to return to work until the Charter became the law of the land. This, argues Foster, was a revolutionary general strike which brought class consciousness to the boil and should have generated a more serious and sustained threat to the established order than it did (Foster, 1974).

Some of the most convincing evidence in opposition to Foster involves the rapid decline in active and visible mass support for the Charter after the failure of the strike. Any wider political class consciousness it engendered must have been at best ephemeral, and the tortuous and convoluted ways in which Foster attempted to explain this dissolution suggest that he was pushing his original argument further than the evidence would allow. In any case, it is harder to find evidence of conviction and commit-ment below the level of those relatively skilled trades which could afford to collect subscriptions, combine and strike. It is not neces-sary to subscribe to the cruder and angrier of the attacks on Foster's work, which reduced people's motives to economic terms in far more distorting ways than Foster's Marxism ever did, to accept that his presentation of the great strike is romantically overblown (Foster, 1974).

What Chartism did achieve in its strongholds, however, was to pull together whole industrial communities in support of the common cause (Calhoun, 1982). These were mainly but not entirely working class in their social structure, with a few employers and an admixture of the *petite bourgeoisie*. In places like Sabden, an industrial village in the Pennines near Pendle Hill where sales of the *Northern Star* reached saturation point, or Todmorden where even the leading manufacturers who domin-ated the local economy were actively sympathetic to the Charter (Weaver, 1987), Chartism at its peak represented the fears and aspirations of whole chapel congregations, friendly society lodges, trade union locals and singing-saloon devotees. It built on a thriving associational culture and pulled together a 'union of the productive classes', uniting the insecure middle ranks (R.S. Neale's 'middling class', in his enduringly useful formula) of small shop-keepers and marginal professionals with the workers in defence against doctrinaire policies which threatened to destabilize their family economies (Neale, 1968). As Feargus O'Connor was well aware, the key division was between the comfortable middle class, the beneficiaries of 1832, and their social inferiors, rather than between middle class and working class broadly and coarsely defined; and the 'rough' working class of drink and deference had little to do with Chartist activism, although an overlapping popular culture of drink and disrespect was a widespread contrib-utor to the movement, despite the best efforts of teetotal and 'knowledge' Chartists. But the kind of 'class consciousness' that pulled together wage-earners against the rest of society, in pursuit of a revolution which would overturn property and topple employers, was not at issue here, despite the importance of the organized trades in Chartism (which derived much of its local complexion from the dominant manufactures) and despite the evidence that many small traders and schoolteachers were actu-ally blacklisted former operatives.

Chartism added up the older radicalisms and something more, because its support was pulled together by a range of hopes and fears which had been crystallized more sharply than ever before by the post-Reform parliaments and the sense of betrayal engen-dered by the harvest of 1832. Its activists were drawn disproportionately from a generation born at the beginning of the nineteenth century, whose formative adult years had seen the reform and trade union campaigns of the post-Waterloo period; and it was among these experienced, embittered but still hopeful thirtysomethings that Chartism came closest to predominance (Godfrey, 1979 pp. 189–236). Partly as a result, Chartist speakers and the Chartist press spoke the languages of principled opposi-tion to 'Old Corruption' and the aristocratic state; but alongside this inherited rhetoric, with differing emphases and occasional conflicts in varying contexts, there was a powerful admixture of antagonism towards middle-class abuse of property and power, which issued forth in denunciations of economic exploitation and the denial of workers' rights, and sometimes in a kind of socialism. Chartism could be, and sometimes was, about class conflict. The word 'class' is pervasive in Chartist speeches and writings, although the fault-line usually ran between the lower middle and comfortable middle classes rather than between employers and workpeople or rich and poor. But whether the predominant critique of current arrangements was political or economic in inspiration and goals, the movement was capable of organizing impressively and on the grand scale, and of generating a rhetoric which combined the violent and the apocalyptic with appeals to reason and fairness. Too much has been made of the alleged dichotomy between physical force and moral force. But it is time to move on from Chartist goals to Chartist actions, exploring this and related issues in greater depth.

# 3

# Chartist Strategies

## Chartist Moderation

Although it is possible to find ample evidence of socialist and revolutionary calls to arms in the enormous printed output of the movement, what impresses most on balance is the moderation and constitutionality of most mainstream Chartist proposals, despite the fierce rhetoric and socialist influences of (for example) Bronterre O'Brien, Richard Pilling, Richard Marsden, Peter Murray McDouall, or, in the later stages of the movement, Ernest Jones (Kirk, 1987; Saville, 1952). There was some contact with Marx and Engels, especially by G.J. Harney and later Jones himself, as well as assorted legacies from earlier versions of socialism, revolutionary or otherwise. But Chartism was, above all, a petitioning movement for the redress of grievances, which was a deeply traditional and (in principle, as some Chartists complained) even deferential way of proceeding. Admittedly, it was compelled to take this route by the illegality of other strategies, and the presentation of a single monster petition was a way of avoiding the rejection of more specific petitions under new rules in the House of Commons, as had happened to a petition for the repeal of the New Poor Law in February 1838. Radicals had become disillusioned with petitioning, which is why repeated assurances were made that 'this' would be the last great petition to end them all; but despite this world-weariness, and the way in which petitioning was used as a cloak to legitimize other

activities, the nature of the tactics used coloured the wider char-
acter of Chartism as a whole (Epstein, 1982).

Chartism was also in some important senses a reactive movement, impelled more by fears and pressures than by positive (or
at least articulated) hopes and dreams or utopian visions of an
alternative society, despite the legacy of Owenism in some places.
It might almost be regarded as a counter-revolutionary movement in many of its guises, seeking to reverse the forward march
of free trade and the dismantling of protective legislation and
assumptions which had been such a feature of the 1820s and
1830s, if anything gathering momentum after the Reform Act.
Much of it was anti-Malthusian, anti-Benthamite and opposed
to expansion of the administrative and policing (and indeed
taxing) powers of central government, although the London
Working Men's Association and the middle-class leadership of
the Birmingham Political Union were much more sympathetic
to the Whig reformers. In important ways Chartism as it developed, and especially with regard to its popular following, might
be defined in terms of what it was not, of an 'other' which might
be summed up as the modernizing project of an emergent industrial state, although one of Chartism's problems was that it was
also directed against the traditional corruption associated with
the landed aristocracy. The monstrous 'other' with which it
contended (a lineal descendant of the 'Thing' denounced by
William Cobbett) was actually two-headed, and the heads faced
in opposite directions. But the importance within Chartism of
appeals to tradition (as in the idealized Anglo-Saxon constitution,
although allusions to this were declining in importance in the
post-Cobbett era of the later 1830s), and of the inherited language
of constitutional purification, gave the movement a Tory traditionalist as well as a latter-day Jacobin flavour; and Tory radicals
like Richard Oastler were vociferous in their criticisms of Whig
political economy when they contributed in apocalyptic language
to (especially) the factory reform and anti-New Poor Law movements which fed into Chartism. Feargus O'Connor and others
were prepared to work with the grain of this Tory radical
strain in the early days of the movement, as the apocalyptic
rhetoric of Oastler and the less readily classifiable Joseph Rayner
Stephens helped to pull the Factory Reform and anti-New
Poor Law campaigns of the industrializing North into Chartism, adopting languages of religious fervour and attaching the

threatened multitudes to Chartism even as the orators themselves became distanced from it. These connections did not make O'Connor into some kind of Tory fellow-traveller, although he remained on friendly terms with Oastler for the rest of his life; but they did provide an extra dimension of religious tradition-alism to the torchlight meetings and other mass gatherings of the movement's earliest days in the North, to be set against the more rationalistic and conventionally 'respectable' London artisan culture from which the Charter had emerged.

## Chartism and the Constitution

In spite of the dangerously revolutionary connotations of its Conventions (as parallel parliaments offering alternative legit-imacy), Chartism's characteristic weapon was the petition to parliament, which it was hoped would carry the day by the sheer moral force of its constitutional logic, without needing to be backed by the physical force of an outraged people, although this was a threat which could be held in reserve and alluded to in more or less veiled ways by Chartist orators. This was an approach founded in medieval precedent, evoking the sort of romantic appeal to tradition which had called in misty reminiscences of an imaginary Anglo-Saxon democracy to the service of parliamen-tary reform campaigns. Chartists were, of course, highly conscious of the radical traditions to which they themselves were heir, commemorating reformers from Thomas Paine to Major Cartwright to Henry Hunt (whose mantle Feargus O'Connor ostentatiously claimed) in various ways from routine rhetorical homage to birthday dinners, displaying veteran radicals on the platform of meetings and electing them to prominent positions, and celebrating the anniversaries of the Peterloo Massacre of 1819, while cultivating and glorying in the possibility that they them-selves might have to wear the martyr's crown if government took a similarly repressive road. This was still a society which respected traditions (even those of recent invention) and used them to vali-date actions; and Chartist leaders knew how to make use of such sentiments and expectations.

It was in keeping with this respect for an idealized ancient constitution and for the power of tradition that Chartism itself did not make a direct attack on the House of Lords (apart from the presence of the bishops there), or even on the monarchy.

John Saville is right to draw attention to a popular republican tradition which idealized the United States of America and interacted with Chartism as well as running parallel to it, and there was also the 'Jacobin' strand of supporters of an idealized version of the first French Revolution (Saville, 1987). Moreover, Richard Williams points out that (for example) the *Northern Star*'s professed love of and loyalty to Queen Victoria was conditional on her being seen to rule on behalf of all her people. The Chartist press was quick to criticize royal extravagance and connections with 'Old Corruption' (R. Williams, 1997 pp. 16–19). Chartist rhetoric was deployed in particularly scathing style against a third pillar of the constitution, the Church of England. A trawl through the Chartist press found a consistent pattern of denunciation of the Church as fraudulent, corrupt, exploitative and hypocritical, and there was almost complete unanimity on the need to separate Church and state, with widespread support for the nationalization of Church property and the abolition of tithes and church-rates, the much-resented compulsory taxes which the Church levied, supposedly for the upkeep of clergy and buildings. Conspicuous Chartist invasions of church services *en masse* were a particular feature of the summer of 1839, as Chartists sought to display their numerical strength publicly and legally and to criticize the Church's opposition to the movement. But Chartism favoured a social and charitable version of Christianity, and the rhetoric of its speeches and journalism was steeped in religious imagery: atheists and freethinkers were a minority within the ranks. Opposition was less to the Church of England (and the Wesleyans, who were also denounced in vituperative language) in principle, than to the conservative and repressive politics with which these denominations were identified; and the Church was not a high priority in the list of Chartist grievances (Faulkner, 1970 pp. 28–39). The movement also respected private property, despite the scarifying rhetoric which was often deployed against those who misused their possessions and power to exploit others and defined their ownership in terms of rights without responsibilities. Even the Chartist Land Plan assumed that the plots on which the escapers from industrial society would be settled would be purchased in due form through a legally constituted company. There was no question of seizing or occupying land owned by others, even if it was lying fallow. This reflected a general respect within the movement for the principles of the rule of law and the jury system, and Chartists recognized the importance of working within the law even as they strained the tolerance of its enforcers to their limits and challenged them to go beyond them. This point is developed in the next chapter.

Also significant were the Chartists who were attracted into sub-movements which emphasized individual self-improvement, such as 'Teetotal Chartism' and the array of initiatives which were derisively summed up as 'Education Chartism', especially those which were connected with William Lovett's 'New Move' in 1841 (Wiener, 1989; B. Harrison, 1973). Part of the sub-text here was an assumption that (in practice) the vote might have to be 'earned' rather than claimed as of right, and that outward and visible signs of respectability might be necessary to convince the authorities that the working classes were 'ready' to be entrusted with this responsibility. This did not impress parliamentarians like the Whig historian Macaulay, whose fear of the consequences of letting the unpropertied come within the pale of the constitution on equal terms was too ingrained to be mollified by conventional evidence of respectability (D. Thompson, 1984 p. 237). There was also a tendency in similar Chartist circles to assume that society could only be reformed through the sum of individual self-improvement, rather than by collective action to right the wrongs of economic and social systems; and these assumptions slotted in much better with prevailing orthodoxies about individualism, free trade and evangelical religion than did the socialist ideas which were also present in the broad church of Chartism.

Republicanism remained a fringe creed within the Chartist movement, more a warning of the lengths to which frustration might lead than a serious part of the practical agenda. In 1839 the Convention adjourned, with no serious opposition, to see the Queen open parliament, and subsequently the *Northern Star* consistently brought its weight to bear against republican tendencies (Mather, 1980 pp. 24, 70–2). By the same token, socialism was never part of the Chartist mainstream in the movement's heyday, although it became much more influential in the declining years after 1848, when the stars of G.J. Harney and Ernest Jones were in the ascendant in a darker firmament (Mather, 1980 p. 32). Interestingly, the socialist critiques of capitalist society which had been developing in the 1820s, and were still being developed in newspapers such as the *Poor Man's Guardian* in the

mid-1830s, petered out during the Chartist years, although industrial employers as capitalists came in for sustained denunciation
through the Chartist press (Saville, 1987 pp. 214–15). Occasional
republican, socialist or anti-clerical utterances provided justifications for the fears of the Chartists' opponents, and were publicized
accordingly, and which led the Complete Suffrage Union to urge
that the label 'Chartist' had become a liability by 1842. But this
smacked more of media scaremongering than of a faithful representation of Chartist goals and strategies.

## Chartism and Insurrection

In many ways, then, as Mather suggests, Chartism was 'at heart,
a very English movement', in the conventional senses attached
to that phrase: traditionalist, constitutionalist, even royalist
(Mather, 1980 p. 24). But it also had an insurrectionary mode of
expression, especially at times of maximum frustration and
economic hardship, which at times and in places became associated with actual plans for armed uprisings in pursuit of its
constitutional goals. It is not helpful to analyse the movement's
activities and internal divisions solely in terms of a dichotomy
between 'moral force' and 'physical force'. This has been a
common strategy in historical writing, which since the pioneering
work of Hovell has tended to attach the former label to the
'moderates' of the London Working Men's Association and the
'New Move', characterized as respectable artisans, and the latter
to Feargus O'Connor and the 'unskilled', violent, emotional
radicals of the East London Democratic Association and the
north of England, characterized as unscrupulous demagogue and
ignorant dupes. In fact, 'moral force' always needed the threat
of insurrection in the background to give it credibility, while
'physical force' needed the legitimization which could only be
provided by the visible exhaustion of all alternative routes. They
were broad bands along a shifting continuum, rather than polar
opposites, and this helps to explain why William Lovett, for
example, could be indicted and convicted for his vocal support
for the Manifesto of Ulterior Measures in 1839 (Wiener, 1989
pp. 66–7). But rejecting this over-simplification should not blind
us to the existence, at various times, of insurrectionary tendencies within Chartism, which were indeed associated with the East
London Democrats and with those northern manufacturing

districts which were most angrily opposed to the New Poor Law and where O'Connor's star shone brightest.

The East London Democratic Association predated the Charter itself. It was founded in 1837 on Tom Paine's birthday, 29 January, part of the general ferment of radical activity out of which Chartism coalesced. On 10 August 1848 it broadened its remit as the London Democratic Association. Its founders represented a variety of strands of older East End radicalism, including insurrectionary ones; and its leading figure, Harney, was identified with both 'Jacobin' and 'levelling' tendencies, combining political and economic egalitarianism. Its organization used French Revolution terminology ('tribunes'), and it set social goals firmly alongside political ones, opposing the London Working Men's Association (which became its rival) by campaigning against the New Poor Law and supporting trade unions, and adopting the socialist doctrines which had become current in the 1820s. It emphasized its openness to working men of all backgrounds, including the poor and others outside the charmed circle of the 'respectable' trades and crafts, and seems to have appealed especially to artisans in the 'dishonourable' trades, whose wages and conditions were being forced down by untrammelled competition. Francis Place, who was contemptuous of its views, described the Association's members as 'the most outrageous of those who preached violence in almost every form', and it developed a reputation as a ferment of violent rhetoric and insurrectionary activity. There was something in this, but it was not so simple. Many Democrats did envisage an uprising as the last in a series of measures to wrest control from the existing parliament in the name of the Convention of 1839, and to this end they advocated arming and drilling. They drew analogies with the French Revolution, especially during the transition to the Republic in 1792–3, and thereby showed a willingness to step outside the English constitutionalism which was general in the movement, although arming and drilling could be justified in terms of the ancient right of the English citizen to bear arms, especially in resistance to acts of tyranny. It was thus that an insurrection was expected to begin. When it came to the crunch, however, the status of all the fiery rhetoric about armed defence became problematic. The Democrats were aware of spies in their midst, and when risings were threatened at the turn of 1839–40 they seem to have set up a diversion, threatening an uprising in London to prevent troops from being sent outside the capital to the other trouble-spots. But even this is speculation, and their activities appear almost as an elaborate game, winding up the authorities in the hope of provoking excessive reactions. In practice it proves impossible to link up incendiary rhetoric and genuine revolutionary capacity or intent, and this is a widespread problem in the sources (Bennett, in Epstein and Thompson (eds), 1982 pp. 87–119).

In general, insurrection was more a rhetorical strategy than a genuine intent even among the most outspoken Chartists. There were moments when it was genuinely considered, and even when efforts were made to orchestrate a rising beyond the local level, at the crest of each surge of Chartist activity, in 1839–40, 1842 and 1848. Such initiatives took place when it became clear that petitioning backed up by the symbolism of marches and mass meetings had failed to deliver the goods; and they were concentrated into industrial areas which were suffering particularly severely from the cyclical unemployment, pressure on wages, undermining of established working practices and loss of bargaining power which this particularly traumatic phase of industrialization brought in its wake. But these were aberrant phenomena, and there was never any serious possibility that they could be co-ordinated on a national stage, especially as Chartism was relatively weak in the capital until it was already in decline elsewhere. They cannot be made the basis for generalizations about the characteristics of Chartism in the north, or among the 'unskilled'. Nor, it seems clear, can they be associated with Feargus O'Connor, who was playing a dangerous but different game.

## Feargus O'Connor

Miles Taylor sums up the situation:

> Chartism did not profess revolutionary aims. The movement's preferred strategy of platform agitation – shows of strength by mass demonstration, anti-parliaments, and national conventions – all belonged to a tradition of moral, constitutionalist pressure which had been the hallmark of radical politics since the eighteenth century.
>
> (Miles Taylor, 1995 p. 100)

O'Connor operated firmly within this tradition, and in the related idiom of the gentlemanly demagogue, expounding the rights and needs of a popular constituency in a paternalist way (as witness the frequent claims on the loyalty of audiences as 'my children', and the offers to risk and even sacrifice his life and liberty for their well-being). An Irish landowner and barrister, he had emerged on the English radical political scene through campaigns for the repeal of the union between Britain and Ireland and against Irish church and other taxation issues, and through his candidature for the Commons in the turbulent cotton-town constituency of Oldham at a by-election in 1835. He was a romantic, emotional orator, whose speeches were said to sound much better than they read; but he stopped short of being carried away into advocating insurrection, and when it came to the crunch his *Northern Star*, the national mouthpiece of the movement, was blunt in its discouragement of armed uprisings. O'Connor was a keen advocate of Chartism as a working-class movement, making no concessions to more moderate reformers from the comfortably-off middle class (though shopkeepers might be a different matter), and the National Charter Association, in which he was so influential, has been claimed as the first working-class political party; and in this sense, perhaps, he acted as a bridge between the older radicalisms and the new. But what he was not, was a revolutionary; and Marxist historians have criticized him for not going far enough. Nor, indeed, was he in any sense a socialist. The movement's most difficult problems, and those of O'Connor himself, arose from the contradictions inherent in stirring up enthusiasm through potent rhetoric, while stopping short of advocating an insurrection which seemed bound to fail; and this posed impossible questions when the constitutional modes of agitation had been exhausted. He, more than any other individual, was the enduring mouthpiece of Chartism nationally, while working continually to sustain and encourage the localities which were its lifeblood; but as part of this process he had to listen to the opinions of others, to keep his finger on the pulse of the movement, and to adjust his programme accordingly. Leadership was about negotiation (Epstein, 1982; Epstein in Ashton, Fyson and Roberts (eds), 1995).

# The Languages of Chartism

O'Connor's language, like that of most Chartist spokesmen, was suffused with romantic and biblical imagery. It spoke to the cultural expectations of people who had come through Sunday Schools and the much-maligned (because beyond the control of either the state or organized religion) 'dame schools', and who were in many cases self-educated by reading what came to hand and discussing their ideas through mutual improvement societies or public-house gatherings. They filled the *Northern Star* with poetry which now looks overblown and grandiloquent, but which reflected the literature which provided their role models (Roberts in Ashton, Fyson and Roberts (eds), 1995). Alongside it, however, was an oral culture of melodrama and ballad, which also assumed a language of heightened emotion, drama and black-and-white morality and encouraged its participants to think in terms of villains and heroes, seducers and victims, luxurious vice and honest toil. This helped to generate a florid rhetoric which looks much more violent and threatening in retrospect than it actually was in the context of the time, and whose content varied in emphasis according to audience as well as theme. There were, in short, many languages of Chartism, and ideas about class, the rights of the people and the oppression of corrupt government were likely to be expressed through the idioms of (for example) melodrama or the sermon. This confused contemporary middle-class readers and listeners as much as it does historians, and Dorothy Thompson rightly draws attention to the veil of conventional expectation through which the comfortably off and conventionally educated obtained a dim and distorted (and therefore frightening) view of Chartist political culture. The languages of Chartism need to be read not only carefully, but also with an eye to context, and that includes the meaning of Feargus O'Connor's ostentatious wearing of a fustian suit (the cheap and uncomfortable cloth in which working men were clad), the languages of gesture and the symbolism of the seating arrangements at meetings. There is much to be done in this vein (Joyce, 1991; D. Thompson, 1984 pp. 237–70; Pickering, 1995).

What is clear is that Chartism had social as well as political goals, and that it is as artificial to divorce them as it is to insist on a simple dichotomy between 'physical force' and 'moral force'. It had, after all, a very broad agenda, extending to foreign policy in the sense of building bridges to democratic movements else-where (a goal which attracted more sympathy in some sections of the movement than in others) (Jones, 1975 pp. 159–70). It cannot be summed up in terms of a narrowly political agenda, however fecund and enduring the traditions on which it built. But its political programme and identity were at the core of its being, and nowhere is this more importantly expressed than through an analysis of Chartism's relationship with government and the state.

# 4

# Repression and Concession: the state and Chartism

## Chartism and the Law

Explanations for the decline and fall of Chartism have often focused on the extravagance and impossibility of its political goals in the context of the time, on the personalities of the leaders, and on the disputes and splits which fragmented the movement. What needs more attention is the nature, strength and (as it turned out) adaptability of the forces against which the Chartists were pitted: the power of the state not only to coerce, censor, repress, make propaganda and deny the space in which to act, but also to set the agenda, to calibrate responses and to present itself as responding modestly and responsibly to those grievances which it chose to recognize as legitimate. It is convenient but dangerous to write about the state as if it were a person with a will and capacity to make choices of its own, and we need to remember the complexity of the system of power, the variety of levels at which it operated (from the individual magistrate in the locality to the central organs of national government) and the scope for conflict and transition within them. Nevertheless, discussing the role of the state in resisting and defeating Chartist goals provides a useful route to understanding the processes at work. But it is also important to remember that our perceptions of the processes of curtailment, control, intimidation, punishment and judicious concession are coloured by the general assumptions that the British state of the 1830s and 1840s was a legitimate body, and that its laws deserved to be obeyed even by those who experienced some of them as oppressive and sought to change them. Most Chartists, most of the time, behaved as if they themselves subscribed to these assumptions, although not uncritically:

> The Chartists were acutely sensitive to the discrepancy between constitutionality and legality (when the law was made by corrupt factions), but none the less they wanted not only to be impeccably constitutional ... but also if possible to remain legal as well.
> (Yeo, in Epstein and Thompson (eds), 1982 p. 360)

Laws might be made constitutionally but introduced and interpreted in the interests of 'corrupt factions', but they should still be obeyed if Chartism was to lay claim to the moral superiority which underpinned its identity.

At a strategic level, many of Chartism's problems arose from the way in which the movement sought to agitate constitutionally, accepting the established conventions while striving to strain them to the uttermost and to provoke their rulers into losing legitimacy by breaching them in their turn. Working within the letter of specific laws had a more pragmatic dimension, making the movement's leaders and organization less vulnerable both to direct legal attack and to accusations of defying constituted authority. Behaving in these ways was a hallmark of Chartist respectability, and it is important that no frontal assault was made on the legitimacy of the constitution, or on the observance of the laws as they currently stood, however bitterly they might be criticized for systematic unfairness. Chartism might have challenged the whole constitutional and legal structure, root and branch, as happened in revolutionary France; and it would also be open to historians to do so. Most historians have declined this option, usually without discussion; but the legitimacy of the early industrial state was questionable, even after Reform, and this is a hidden context for the choices Chartists made. It is important that Chartism, as a movement, did not go down this continental road of thoroughgoing denial and defiance: that it took the existing constitution as a given and conducted its business within the resulting framework of shared assumptions. This was a key element in Chartism's perceived 'Englishness'; and it both limited

Chartism's freedom of movement, and limited the extent to which it could be persecuted and suppressed by a state which needed to sustain the image of legality, due process and moderation by which it justified its exercise of power. As Edward Thompson pointed out, the rise of new social forces from the late eighteenth century to challenge the aristocratic constitution, which rested on assumptions about the majesty, justice and mercy of the law as a shared resource, presented Britain's rulers with

> ... alarming alternatives. They could either dispense with the rule of law, dismantle their elaborate constitutional structures, countermand their own rhetoric and exercise power by force; or they could submit to their own rules and surrender their hegemony. In the campaign against Paine and the printers, in the Two Acts (1795), the Combination Acts (1799–1800), the repression of Peterloo (1819) and the Six Acts (1820) they took halting steps in the first direction. But in the end, rather than shatter their own self-image and repudiate 150 years of constitutional legality, they surrendered to the law.
>
> (E.P. Thompson, 1975 p. 269)

It was, nevertheless, a law which they controlled and which they could manipulate in their own interests; and working according to its requirements made life difficult for the Chartists in important ways. Moreover, the legislation Thompson refers to (and more besides) was still on the statute book, available for reactivation, and awareness of this affected Chartism's room for manoeuvre, even (perhaps especially) where the actual scope of the law was ambiguous and open to interpretation by judges. Where the exercise of 'physical force' by the state was concerned, too, Chartists were haunted by the possibility of a repeat of the Peterloo massacre, although fear of the propaganda value of such an occurrence also restrained local and national authorities at crucial points, not least in dealing with the great strike of August 1842, whose peak (in Manchester itself) coincided with a well-publicized Peterloo anniversary (Jenkins, 1980 pp. 80–1, 152–5). But, in the last resort, the metropolitan police and the military were always available to corral and overawe strikers and demonstrators, and ultimately, when the time was ripe or the immediate threat became intolerable, to charge, strike, shoot and break up the crowds. The Chartists were never able to win over the police or the army to their cause.

## Chartist Organizations

At a more everyday level which matters a great deal, we have already encountered the problems of organization which arose from interpretations of the legislation against corresponding societies and seditious meetings, and on the registration of friendly societies and other voluntary bodies. Chartists sought to set up organizations which were as inclusive and democratic as possible, while being capable of acting at national as well as local level. Such seemingly simple goals were beset by practical problems: poverty made it difficult to keep up subscriptions; office-holders were more likely to be drawn from a limited group of those who had some control over their time and security of employment, but this raised the spectre of creating elite cadres within the movement which corroded the ideal of participant democracy; and there was sustained resistance to the payment of officials, lecturers and 'missionaries'. This did not prevent such full-time posts from being established but did create an atmosphere of suspicion and parsimony (but how much *should* such a necessary representative of a movement of the poor and excluded be paid?). Beyond all this the law created problems of its own. The Seditious Meetings Act of 1817 forbade (on pain of seven years' transportation) the setting up of societies which acted together through correspondence or other concerted communication, and of societies which had branches with separate officials. As Yeo remarks, 'What was illegal was just what the Chartists wanted – a national movement which still allowed for a large measure of local autonomy and control.' Freemasons, religious and charitable societies, approved friendly societies (after 1846) and societies approved by the magistrates in Quarter Sessions were exempt, but these routes were closed off to the Chartists. To make matters worse, without legal recognition Chartist organizations had no way of recovering funds at law if (for example) a treasurer absconded. A great deal of energy and ingenuity was expended throughout the Chartist years in trying to devise structures which met legal requirements: this applied to the size and forms of election of the Conventions, the organization of the National Charter Association, and the Land Plan, and yet the state's legal mouthpieces and bureaucrats (especially John Tidd Pratt, the Registrar of Friendly Societies) always came up with restrictive definitions of the law. The uncertain legality of Chartist bodies itself generated strife within the movement, as some refused to join organizations they feared to be illegal, or used such fears as an excuse for holding aloof. Lovett's estrangement from the National Charter Association is a case in point. In a sense, the government did not need to institute heavy-handed and controversial prosecutions of Chartist organizations: most of the work was done for it by the reputation for power which the law afforded, and the ambiguities it entailed (Yeo, in Epstein and Thompson (eds), 1982 pp. 360–74).

## Sedition and Repression

Nor did government hold aloof from new measures, however. The power to arrest, remand in custody and prosecute orators and journalists for ill-defined offences involving sedition or incitement was a serious curb on what could be said, especially given the scope for misrepresentation by biased witnesses, but it was also expanded in the crisis of 1848. The Crown and Security Act of April in that year (better known as the 'Treason–Felony Act') reduced the applicability of the offence of high treason to direct offences against the sovereign, turning other kinds of treason into ordinary felonies (and removing the awesome threat of hanging, drawing and quartering convicted offenders). To these felonies, however, was added that of 'open and advised speaking' against monarch and constitution; and this made it easier to secure jail sentences against Chartist orators, as a spate of successful prosecutions during 1848–9 made clear. The judges who heard trials of this kind displayed an unnerving unanimity in sternly rejecting the legitimacy of Chartist opinions; and this development enhanced the state's existing power to limit free speech by the threat of prosecution (Saville, 1987 pp. 170–3). The imprisonment of Chartist leaders after each of the movement's peaks of activity did provide a rallying-point for campaigns to petition for pardons, and opportunities for demonstrations of solidarity when prisoners were released, providing attainable goals which helped to hold the movement together in difficult times; but this was small consolation.

The legal problems Chartism encountered have given rise to interesting speculation about the changing nature of the movement after the 1842 strikes and the ensuing trials. John Foster and Mick Jenkins argued that the government's retreat from the original intention to conduct 'a monster show trial that would conclusively and publicly demonstrate that the leaders of organized labour and of the Chartist movement had conspired together to overthrow the state' marked a significant and enduring change of attitude which also affected the Chartist leadership (Jenkins, 1980 p. 16). Local leaders of the strike and agitation had been summarily and often harshly dealt with by Special Commissions in the strike's aftermath, and at first Sir James Graham, the Home Secretary, intended to try O'Connor and the Manchester delegates to the NCA conference in August for high treason, and then to indict them for seditious conspiracy before the Court of Queen's Bench in London. What eventually happened was much less dramatic. O'Connor and 58 others were brought before the spring assizes at Lancaster in 1843, but the trial was conducted in a relaxed way, and 'both judge and jury behaved with remarkable leniency' (Epstein, 1982 p. 301). Jenkins argues that the evidence of Richard Pilling was highlighted in such a way as to make the defendants seem driven by hunger, deprivation and spontaneous anger against hard-hearted masters, rather than (much more damningly) by political principle. This was, as Jenkins shows, a complete distortion of Pilling's long career as outspoken Chartist activist: his speech at the trial presented him as a simple, wronged working man, and this elicited the requisite sympathy. The outcome was that the 1842 strikes were presented as much less threatening than Graham acknowledged them to have been at the time, and in a way that distorted subsequent historical interpretation: they were belittled in order to reduce their power, just as the prisoners were allowed to escape through loopholes in the law. Thus the trial was 'managed' in a way that allowed the defendants to present themselves in as harmless a light as possible, while enabling the government to avoid the creation of martyrs and opening the way to concessions on a broader front. Foster argues that as part of this process, 'The judge made it his special task to provide a particularly broad definition of legitimate political agitation, and Feargus O'Connor then accepted this as the basis of a "covenant" binding on all future Chartist activity' (Jenkins, 1980 pp. 16 and 107–27). This ensured that there would be no recurrence of the alliance between Chartism and organized labour which had so frightened the authorities in August and September 1842.

This interpretation smacks unduly of implausible conspiracy, and direct evidence for its key themes is lacking. Nor does it do justice to the strength of the Chartist challenge in 1848, although it took a different form (and was in its turn belittled by a very successful media campaign, which has also influenced historians unduly) (Saville, 1987 pp. 200–4). What it does underline, however, is the power of the government to set the agenda and tone for its efforts at repression by deciding the time, place and indictment of the trial, and the limitations placed upon its actions by the need to avoid exacerbating tensions, creating martyrs and (above all) undermining its own legitimacy by palpable unfairness or vindictiveness. This was the outcome of a long learning process which does seem to have reached a turning-point in the Lancaster trial. But what is also noticeable is the power the prisoners had to decide on their own rhetorical and legal strategies, which could themselves affect the outcome. Resources were undoubtedly uneven, but the law at this level was available to both sides, though (as we saw above) more accessibly and flexibly in 1843 when outcomes were still in doubt than in 1848–9 when Chartism had clearly been defeated.

## The Softening of the State?

The notion that the attitude of the state began to soften after 1843, and that it began to make legislative and administrative concessions to Chartist grievances, remains a useful way of approaching an explanation for the decline of Chartism, however suspicious we may be of the details of the Foster/Jenkins thesis. It was at this point that the Peel government began to be more sympathetic to factory reform, and the economic reforms of mid-decade were also calculated to take the pressure off working–class living standards. As Stedman Jones suggests, Chartism's rhetoric in its early years was directed against a state which recognized and protected all kinds of property but those of labour and skill, and which seemed to be waging war on working-class living standards and institutions through a series of measures which excluded working people from local and national political processes, and threatened them with oppression and control

71

through (for example, and most obviously) the New Poor Law and the new police. Chartism inherited and deployed the assumption that the state was irredeemably corrupt, colonized by those who were able to exploit their unchecked political power for private gain, and that under the current political system all legislative initiatives would be turned to the account of the landed aristocracy and 'moneyocracy', and used for the further exploitation and repression of the wage-earning and taxpaying majority (Stedman Jones, in Epstein and Thompson (eds), 1982; Miles Taylor, 1995 p. 5).

Developments in the early and mid-1840s undermined these assumptions. The New Poor Law proved to be less threatening in practice than the rhetoric of its introduction had suggested, especially in the northern factory districts where it took a very long time for new workhouses to be built or new officials to be appointed (Midwinter, 1969). The burden of taxation began to shift from necessary consumables to property and substantial incomes, especially as local graduated property taxes took up the financial burden of urban improvement as well as poor relief. Movement began at last on the factory reform issue, with the 'Ten Hours Bill' visibly becoming attainable by mid-decade and legislation in 1847 and 1850 bringing it in. The Corn Laws were repealed in 1846, and Chartists soon came to acknowledge their benefits in the new, more benign climate of government. Prosecutions of trade unionists faded into the background. Reformism became credible because reforms were under way. The state was no longer necessarily the enemy, and this sea-change was taking place without the thoroughgoing democratic reform which Chartism held to be indispensable. There were two ironies. The most obvious area of policy in which government reverted to the classic 1830s mixture of coercion and *laissez-faire*, after the fall of Peel in 1846, was the Irish famine; and the horrific results of this return to earlier orthodoxies helped to recruit a new generation of angry Irish repealers to the Chartist cause in 1848. Moreover, while the state was softening its stance in so many areas of social and economic policy, it continued to build up the police forces, barracks, telegraph networks and other technologies of control which were to make it easier to suppress the last Chartist upsurge in 1848 (Saville, 1987; Mather, 1959). Chartism rose to popularity as a conduit of popular grievances against an array of abusive legislation and interference with

72

working-class institutions and survival strategies in the 1830s. It began to decline when these abuses began to be remedied, although what is remarkable is how little it took to remove the impetus from the movement. What is even more remarkable is that the grievance which was not addressed, the introduction of the new police forces, was to be essential to the repression which played its own important part in Chartism's decline. The state gave ground where there was scope for doing so without undermining the prerogatives of property, but it reserved its powers to coerce and control by legal and military discipline; and this combination of flexibility and strength proved very effective in stabilizing the constitution. However, as the next chapter shows, there was more to the story than this.

# 5

# Chartism in Perspective

The role of the state, of coercion, the manipulation of the law and the softening of attitudes and policies towards the working class and those who were excluded from the franchise, plays an important part in explaining the trajectory of Chartism; but it is part of a broader and richer story, and needs to be placed in context. This concluding chapter looks at additional (and inter-related) explanations for the rise and fall of the movement, before moving on to assess the extent to which it might be said to have succeeded (in spite of the obvious failure to obtain any of the emblematic Six Points, which is where evaluations often stop short), and to evaluate its influence in the longer term. We begin by looking at the wider field of explanations for the timing of Chartism's decline, which was itself no simple or clear-cut matter.

The most tempting set of explanations, for many commenta-tors, centres on the economy and living standards. Those who assume that Chartism as a mass movement was essentially a creed of hard times, almost a reflex response to trade depression and the traumas of adjustment to industrial life, tend to adopt this kind of approach, which plays down the importance of radical traditions, cultures and principles and reduces Chartism to nothing more than a struggle for physical survival. Giving living standards the dominant and determining role is demeaning. It is true that Chartism's greatest and most sustained mobilizations occurred in periods of trade depression and wage cuts, but they could not have taken place without the existence of a substantial core of principled activists who were prepared to allocate scarce resources of their own to sustaining the movement's funding, organization and morale. In times of relatively full employment, long working hours set this kind of commitment at a premium, and it is small wonder that so many of Chartism's national leaders were gentlemen or substantial businessmen who had the time, money and education to travel, underwrite, organize and publicize. The briefest glance at the Chartist press shows the sophisticated range of allusion and humour to which readers – and listeners, when pieces were read aloud – were expected to respond. This was, of necessity, a movement of critical thinkers rather than manipulated dupes. Moreover, if Chartism had been simply an automatic response to bad conditions (and if so, why did it take *this* form?), then we might expect it to be strongest in (for example) Liverpool, that 'black spot on the Mersey', or the agricultural areas of southern England where the Captain Swing riots of 1830 had so alarmed the authorities, rather than the manufacturing districts where it was most in evidence (at least until the aftermath of the 1842 strike). And why did the trade depression of 1846–7, which detailed research on the cotton town of Oldham suggests was worse than either of the previous ones, not ignite a similar Chartist upsurge, which was delayed until the next year? (Foster, 1974 p. 205). Economic explanations for Chartism's failure to rekindle after 1848 carry a little more conviction; railway-building and expanding world markets helped to stabilize the early industrial economy, depressions bit less deep and real wage levels began to rise more convincingly. Optimistic arguments for rising real wages before the late 1840s are undermined by the recurrent evidence of abject poverty in trade depressions (Walton, 1992). But even after 1848 the evidence for significantly improved living standards is problematic. Foster points to a change in the composition of the Oldham labour force between 1841 and 1861, with 'labourers and paupers' rising from 7 to 19 per cent of household heads; and he suggests that, 'As a combined result of increasing wage differentials and a sharp rise in the number of low-paid jobs, the real earnings of the bottom half of the labour force actually fell slightly between 1839 and 1859 at a time when those higher up the scale enjoyed quite a sharp rise' (Foster, 1974 pp. 76, 204). Evidence from a wider area of the Lancashire cotton district suggests that money wages in many occupations fell between 1839 and 1850, and when real wages began to rise in the 1850s they did so very slowly and uncertainly until the end of the decade, and not enough to explain a phenomenon as complex as the decline of Chartism; here, in the Black Country and in London it is clear that poverty and insecurity remained endemic among the unskilled and the declining crafts, and that even the skilled were vulnerable to distressing poverty in the event of unemployment, illness or injury. The nature and timing of trends in living standards cannot be reconciled with a simple relationship between increased material comfort and the decline of Chartism (Kirk, 1985 pp. 91–103; Stedman Jones, 1970).

The evidence for a widening gap between the better off and worse off among the working class can be connected with the argument that Chartism declined because the working class was divided by the emergence (or creation) of a new kind of 'labour aristocracy' of the skilled and secure, with its own institutions and a stake in the system, for whom the Charter began to seem an irrelevance. This, too, is difficult to match up with the chronology of Chartism's decline, as it is clearly a longer process which was still working its way through in the 1860s. The transition from craftsmen who regulated admission to their trades and controlled the organization of the workplace to supervisory workers who passed on the employer's commands to subordinate workpeople (from the 'formal' to the 'real' subordination of labour) was certainly not concentrated into the late 1840s and early 1850s, and the timing of such a transition varied widely between trades and industries. By the same token, it is hard to identify the early Co-operative Societies on the model of the Rochdale Pioneers, or the spread of the Friendly Societies, or mutual improvement associations, or even the temperance movement, with particular strata within the working class, although the better off and better educated would be more likely to follow these paths. In any case, the busiest years for Co-operative development came later, while the Friendly Societies were already growing rapidly before the Chartist years. These thrift and mutual aid societies (to label them 'self-help' makes them seem misleadingly individualist) were often part of the repertoire of local Chartist groups, especially NCA branches, and they may well have diverted energies away from the movement into more practical and accessible goals; but we should not make too much of them (Foster, 1974 pp. 221–38; Gorsky, 1998).

A related argument is that of Joyce, who suggested that Chartism's assumptions were those of artisans who were unable to adjust their critique of the existing political and economic system to the rise of factory work and the subordination to and dependence on a master that this produced, leaving space for employers to develop paternalist regimes which attached workpeople to the factory as a kind of extended family, offering treats, amenities like wash-houses and libraries and incorporation into the celebrations of family and firm. This notion of factory paternalism capturing the allegiance of potential Chartists for a kind of neo-feudalism is based on a limited range of examples, however, and it is not clear that it was either new or effective in the 1840s (Joyce, 1980; Dutton and King, 1982; Kirk, 1985 pp. 14–18).

There were other ways in which divisions developed within the working class, most obviously the rise of a popular Protestant constitutionalism in fierce opposition to the Irish Catholics whose numbers increased considerably and controversially in the wake of the potato famine after 1846. But we have seen that the Irish presence, as it became politicized, also brought strength to the last phase of Chartism, although the rise of an Irish nationalist agenda (to which Feargus O'Connor was always sympathetic) may have put staunch Protestants off. By the early 1850s the Irish were visibly competing for jobs in new sectors of the economy in (for example) cotton towns like Stockport, and for some they became scapegoats for low wages and insecurity. To some extent conflicts of this kind were encouraged by the employers as part of a policy of 'divide and rule'; and more generally the later 1840s were marked by a growing drive on the part of the established political parties to gain or recapture the allegiance of working-class activists at a time when there was increasing scepticism about the practicability and even the value of the Charter (Kirk, 1985 pp. 315–18).

Overtures of this sort were made both at local and national political levels. They involved picking up on attractive causes and presenting candidates for local or parliamentary elections who were friendly to factory reform, or campaigns against the New Poor Law (if Tory), or to the disestablishment of the Church of England or a compromise at household suffrage on the parliamentary reform issue (if Liberal). This, of course, is how the softening of government positions on issues which affected Chartists passed into the practical politics of localities; and for those to whom the Charter was a means to other ends as much as, or more than, an end in itself, such initiatives were attractive. In Oldham, for example, the results could be seen in the attachment of former Chartists to the parties of the propertied classes from 1846–7 onwards. Where apathy and disillusionment did not undermine Chartism, these alternative routes to seemingly attainable goals drew its activists into more orthodox channels. This was not solely a top-down process, of course: Whigs and Tories had to reach out to their new constituencies and make concessions. But the outcome was to confine Chartist survival to a principled remnant which, by mid-century, had lost the power to mobilize more widely (Foster, 1974 pp. 207–10).

Some writers have seen Chartism as, in effect, an anomalous episode: an interval in which a more lasting radical frame of mind, later to find a home within the emergent Liberal Party around mid-century, became detached from mainstream politics and found expression in extra-parliamentary agitation. This view emphasizes long-term continuities in popular politics and stresses Chartist concerns with accountability and economy in government, along with the need for Christian humanitarianism and a modicum of intervention to moralize the market and set limits to the exploitation of defenceless labour. The Chartists were liberal crusaders against corruption and waste, under another name and with a particularly assertive rhetoric. After the movement's demise politics reverted to their natural state, pulling people together across class boundaries through shared ties of culture and dependence which attached them to one party or another; and within the Chartist ranks there were always lapsed or potential Tories and Whigs contending in internal strife (Miles Taylor, 1995; Winstanley, 1993; Joyce, 1991). This sits uneasily alongside the view that Chartism inherited the language and cast of thought of a critique of the unreformed constitution, its abuses and their consequences which had its roots in the eighteenth century and could not be adapted to the new circumstances of the 1840s, when the state and its rulers proved capable of responding to popular complaint and yielding ground through ameliorative legislation and relaxed severity (Stedman Jones, 1983). The one approach emphasizes continuity, the other presupposes a sharp change in trajectory and tone at mid-century, just as do Marxist ideas of Chartism as an expression of working-class consciousness which failed to come to fruition and broke apart under a welter of conflicting stresses (Foster, 1974; Kirk, 1985). The balance of the evidence suggests a significant discontinuity at mid-century, with a transition to relative order and stability on the new basis of a more legitimate state, with a more effective machinery of law enforcement and control to back it up. This mid-century transition ushered in an 'age of equipoise': a valuable phrase, because it suggests less simple stolid stability than an equilibrium of countervailing forces: tensions held in balance, rather than a crushing weight of acquiescence and consensus (Burn, 1957). Conflict did not go away: it was managed and channelled, and crucial to this development was the separation of economic and political issues, as trade union struggles were put in a separate sphere from radical politics. At times, and especially in 1842, Chartism had brought the concerns of the workplace into politics, and its strongest threats to established authority had been associated with such campaigns. Now that the state had retreated from threatening workers' organizations, and the New Poor Law no longer brandished the threat of the workhouse before the unemployed worker in every trade depression, the trade unions fought their battles within the system rather than feeling the need to challenge it. So did other groups with particular interests and concerns. This, above all, took the heat out of Chartism.

This is a reminder that Chartism was more than just a political movement, and the recent tendency to reduce it to a set of political goals, and to analyse its language in political terms, is therefore reductive and distorting. How, in any case, does a researcher decide which pieces of linguistic evidence merit close analysis, and what aspects of the movement they represent? But the whole question of the status of language in historical understanding raises issues which cannot be pursued here (Evans, 1997). How we define Chartist goals affects our perception of the movement's success or failure. It did not achieve any of the Six Points, and after its defeat it was almost lost from view for half a century; but without its surging agitation and intermittent threat it is hard to imagine the governments of the 1840s making the concessions they did. Chartism declined, in part, because some of the goals that drew people into the movement had been attained. To ask why Chartism failed is to misunderstand its nature; the interesting questions are about the extent to which it succeeded.

# Bibliography

The literature on Chartism is so extensive that there are now two full-length modern bibliographies. The one edited by J.F.C. Harrison and Dorothy Thompson, *Bibliography of the Chartist Movement 1837–1976* (Hassocks, Sussex, 1978), which included references to manuscript sources, printed primary sources of various kinds and unpublished theses, has recently been supplemented by O. Ashton, R. Fyson and S. Roberts (eds), *The Chartist Movement: A New Annotated Bibliography* (London, 1995). What follows is a list of the most influential works on Chartism, supplemented by works which are referred to or otherwise used in the text, some of which are not directly about Chartism but have helped to influence my ideas about it. Anyone wanting to develop a serious interest in this important theme is referred to the bibliographies, which are particularly useful in helping researchers to follow themes, investigate important individuals, and discover relevant local case-studies.

O. Ashton, R. Fyson and S. Roberts (eds), *The Duty of Discontent: Essays for Dorothy Thompson* (London, 1995). Includes essays on aspects of Chartism.

G.J. Barnsby, *The Working-class Movement in the Black Country* (Wolverhampton, 1977). A detailed Marxist regional study.

J. Belchem, 'Chartism and the trades, 1848–1850', *English Historical Review* 98 (1983), pp. 261–90.

J. Belchem, *Industrialization and the Working Class* (Aldershot, 1990). A survey with a good introductory treatment of Chartism.

J. Belchem (ed.), *Popular Politics, Riot and Labour* (Liverpool, 1992). Contains an excellent chapter on Liverpool Chartism by Moore: see below.

R. Boston, *British Chartists in America* (Manchester, 1971).

A. Briggs (ed.), *Chartist Studies* (London, 1959). Classic pioneering collection of local and thematic studies: set an agenda.

W.L. Burn, *The Age of Equipoise* (London, 1957).

C. Calhoun, *The Question of Class Struggle* (Oxford, 1982). Includes a Lancashire case-study.

J. Charlton, *The Chartists: the First National Workers' Movement* (London, 1997). Disappointing pamphlet in socialist series: poorly articulated and not always accurate.

A. Clark, 'The rhetoric of Chartist domesticity: gender, language and class in the 1830s and 1840s', *Journal of British Studies* 31 (1992).

A. Clark, *The Struggle for the Breeches* (London, 1993). Pugnacious development of the role of women in popular radicalism and culture.

H.I. Dutton and J. King, 'The "cotton tyrants" of north Lancashire', *Social History* 7 (1982). Critique of Joyce (1980), cited below.

H.I. Dutton and J. King, *Ten Per Cent and No Surrender* (Cambridge, 1981). Chartism and the Lancashire industrial disputes of 1853–4.

J. Epstein, *The Lion of Freedom: Feargus O'Connor and the Chartist Movement, 1832–42* (London, 1982). Sympathetic biography which also provides an excellent history of Chartism up to 1842.

J. Epstein, *Radical Expression: Political Language, Ritual and Symbol in England, 1790–1850* (New York and Oxford, 1994). Careful exploitation of the trend to analysing radical (including Chartist) language, broadly interpreted.

J. Epstein and D. Thompson (eds.), *The Chartist Experience* (London, 1982). Essential: excellent collection of essays, including Sykes on trade unions and Stedman Jones's first presentation of his 'languages of Chartism' argument.

Richard Evans, *In Defence of History* (London, 1997). Important introduction to some of the key questions of the nature of history which are highly relevant to debates on Chartism.

H.U. Faulkner, *Chartism and the Churches* (1916, reprinted London, 1970).

M.C. Finn, *After Chartism: Class and Nation in English Radical Politics, 1848–1874* (Cambridge, 1993).

J. Foster, *Class Struggle and the Industrial Revolution* (London, 1974). Famous controversial Leninist case-study, mainly of Oldham. See also Gadian, Musson, Sykes and Winstanley, below.

D. Fraser, *Urban Politics in Victorian England* (Leicester, 1976).

D. Gadian, 'Class consciousness in Oldham and other north-west industrial towns 1830–1850', *Historical Journal* 21 (1978). Contribution to the Foster debate.

R.G. Gammage, *History of the Chartist Movement 1837–1854* (London, reprinted 1969). The original eye-witness account, full of personal vendettas and spleen but clearer on the early years than the later complications.

V.A.C. Gatrell, 'Incorporation and the pursuit of Liberal hegemony in Manchester, 1790–1839', in D. Fraser (ed.), *Municipal Reform and the Industrial City* (Leicester, 1982).

C. Godfrey, 'The Chartist Prisoners, 1839–41', *International Review of Social History* 24 (1979), 189–236. Useful survey of activists.

D. Goodway, *London Chartism, 1838–1848* (Cambridge, 1982). Important study of more than metropolitan significance.

M. Gorsky, 'The growth and distribution of English friendly societies in the early nineteenth century', *Economic History Review* 51 (1998), 498–511. Highly relevant to Chartism's contexts.

R. Gray, 'The deconstruction of the English working class', *Social History* 11 (1986), 363–73. Contribution to the debates initiated by Stedman Jones and Joyce.

A.M. Hadfield, *The Chartist Land Company* (Newton Abbot, 1970).

B. Harrison, 'Teetotal Chartism', *History* 58 (1973).

B. Harrison and P. Hollis, 'Chartism, Liberalism and the life of Robert Lowery', *English Historical Review* 82 (1967), 503–35.

D. Hempton, *Methodism and Politics in British Society 1750–1850* (London, 1984). Useful short section on Methodism and Chartism.

P. Hollis, *The Pauper Press* (Oxford, 1970).

M. Hovell, *The Chartist movement* (Manchester, 1918). The first academic study, whose assumptions reigned misleadingly supreme for many years.

J. Humphries and S. Horrell, 'Women's labour force participation and the transition to the male-breadwinner family, 1790–1865', *Economic History Review* 48 (1995), 89–117. Important to the factory reform and living standards issues.

M. Jenkins, *The General Strike of 1842* (London, 1980). Well-documented, forceful Marxist analysis.

David Jones, *Chartism and the Chartists* (London, 1975). Episodic but some excellent chapters and documents.

David Jones, *The Last Rising: the Newport Insurrection of 1839* (Oxford, 1985). Careful analysis of a key episode.

G. Stedman Jones, *Languages of Class* (London, 1983). Central to the emergence of the 'linguistic turn'.

G. Stedman Jones, *Outcast London* (Oxford, 1970). Of contextual relevance as a brilliant study of casual labour and the sweated trades in London.

P. Joyce, *Visions of the People: Industrial England and the Question of Class 1848–1914* (Cambridge, 1991). Complex but important discussion of the role of class in popular politics, with special reference to Lancashire.

P. Joyce, *Work, Society and Politics* (Brighton, 1980). Argues for the contribution of a 'new paternalism' to Chartism's decline.

T.M. Kemnitz, 'The Chartist Convention of 1839', *Albion* 10 (1978), 152–70.

J. King, *Richard Marsden and the Preston Chartists* (Lancaster, 1981). Lively short biography.

N. Kirk, *The Growth of Working-class Reformism in Mid-Victorian England* (London, 1985). Excellent on the debates over Chartism's decline.

N. Kirk, 'In defence of class', *International Review of Social History* 32 (1987), 2–47. The clearest statement of Marxist opposition to aspects of the 'linguistic turn'.

N. Kirk, *Labour and Society in Britain and the USA*, vol. 1, *Capitalism, Custom and Protest, 1780–1850* (Aldershot, 1994).

T. Koditschek, *Class Formation and Urban Industrial Society: Bradford 1750–1850* (Cambridge, 1990). A voluminous case-study.

W. Lovett and J Collins, *Chartism: A New Organization of the People* (reprinted with an introduction by Asa Briggs, London, 1969).

F.C. Mather, *Chartism and Society* (London, 1980). Sharp insights and a wide range of documentary sources.

F.C. Mather, *Public Order in the Age of the Chartists* (Manchester, 1959). Classic study of the repressive role of government.

E.C. Midwinter, *Social Administration in Lancashire 1830–1860* (Manchester, 1969). Treatment of the new police is highly relevant to Chartism.

K. Moore, '"This Whig and Tory ridden town": popular politics in Liverpool in the Chartist era', in J. Belchem (ed.), *Popular Politics, Riot and Labour* (Liverpool, 1992).

R.J. Morris, *Class and Class Consciousness, 1780–1850* (London, 1979). Thought-provoking introduction.

R.J. Morris, *Class, Sect and Party* (Manchester, 1990). The Leeds middle class in the Chartist period.

A.E. Musson, 'Class struggle and the labour aristocracy', *Social History* 3 (1976), and reply by J. Foster. The most intemperate of the attacks on Foster, coming from a right-wing 'Old Labour' perspective.

R.S. Neale, *Bath: A Social History 1680–1850* (London, 1981). Good chapter on radicalism in the Chartist period.

R.S. Neale, 'Class and class-consciousness in early nineteenth-century England: three classes or five', *Victorian Studies* 12 (1968), 4–32. Innovative approach to class which deserves attention.

T.M. Parssinen, 'Association, convention and anti-parliament in British radical politics, 1771–1848', *English Historical Review* 88 (1973), 504–33.

P.A. Pickering, 'Class without words: symbolic communication in the Chartist movement', *Past and Present* 112 (1986), 144–62.

P.A. Pickering, *Chartism and the Chartists in Manchester and Salford* (London, 1995). Good at recovering the texture of local Chartist activity and the biographies of local activists.

P. Richards, 'The state and early industrial capitalism: the case of the handloom weavers', *Past and Present* 83 (1979), 92–115. Telling critique of a key primary source.

Ruth Richardson, *Death, Dissection and the Destitute* (London, 1988). Vivid demonstration of the importance of the Anatomy Act of 1832 to the climate of fear which helped to nurture Chartism.

T. Rothstein, *From Chartism to Labourism* (London, 1929). Classic, rather schematic Marxist interpretation.

E. Royle, *Chartism* (Harlow, 1980). Useful short primer.

J. Saville, *1848: The British State and the Chartist Movement* (Cambridge, 1987). Excellent reinterpretation of 1848 and how it has been represented by historians.

J. Saville, *The Consolidation of the Capitalist State, 1800–1850* (London, 1994). Short pamphlet on a key theme.

J. Saville, *Ernest Jones, Chartist* (London, 1952). Biography of a key figure in later Chartism, still valuable.

W. Seccombe, *Weathering the Storm* (London, 1993). Background on work, gender, families and living standards.

A.R. Schoyen, *The Chartist Challenge* (London, 1958). Biography of G.J. Harney.

J. Schwarzkopf, *Women in the Chartist Movement* (London, 1991). The first, and very useful, book-length development of this theme.

R. Sykes, 'Some aspects of working-class consciousness in Oldham, 1830–1842', *Historical Journal* 23 (1980). Contribution to the Foster debate.

R. Sykes, 'Physical-force Chartism: the cotton district and the Chartist crisis of 1839', *International Review of Social History* 30 (1985), 207–36.

Miles Taylor, *The Decline of British Radicalism 1847–1860* (Oxford, 1995). Densely textured, full of ideas.

Peter Taylor, *Popular Politics in Early Industrial Britain: Bolton 1825–1850* (Keele, 1995).

T.R. Tholfsen, *Working-class Radicalism in Mid-Victorian England* (London, 1976). Arguments about what followed Chartism.

D. Thompson, *The Early Chartists* (London, 1971). Useful documents.

D. Thompson, *The Chartists* (Aldershot, 1984). Still the best book-length treatment, well written, developing neglected themes and with a clear point of view.

D. Thompson, *Outsiders: Class, Gender and Nation* (London, 1993). Some material on Chartism and many transferable ideas.

E.P. Thompson, *The Making of the English Working Class* (London, 1963). Classic, though coverage effectively stops at early 1830s. Later editions reply to critics. See also Clark, above.

E.P. Thompson, 'The moral economy of the English crowd in the eighteenth century', *Past and Present* 50 (1971), 76–136. Classic presentation of a concept which many think can help with understanding Chartism.

E.P. Thompson, *Whigs and Hunters: The Origin of the Black Act* (London, 1975). Themes in eighteenth-century history, but again with transferable ideas.

E.P. Thompson, *Customs in Common* (London, 1990). A quarry for big transferable ideas, especially 'moral economy'.

G. Timmins, *The Last Shift: the Decline of Hand-loom Weaving in Nineteenth-century Lancashire* (Manchester, 1993). The most thorough and convincing study of this controversial occupational group, though it ignores the political debates.

J. Vernon, *Politics and the People: A Study in English Political Culture, c. 1815–1867* (Cambridge, 1993). Well-researched linguistic approach.

J. Vernon (ed.), *Re-reading the Constitution* (Cambridge, 1996).

J.K. Walton, 'Die Baumwollindustrie und die Arbeiterklasse von Lancashire: Lebensformen, Lebensstandard und Politik in der Region von Manchester, 1770–1860', in K. Ditt and S. Pollard (eds.), *Von der Heimarbeit in die Fabrik* (Paderborn, 1992). Links the standard of living debate with Chartism.

J.K. Walton, *Lancashire: A Social History 1558–1939* (Manchester, 1987). Regional study which looks critically at debates on Chartism.

J.T. Ward, *Chartism* (London, 1973). Very thorough but blinkered by cynical Tory attitudes to Chartist motives. Often strong on detail but some caution needed.

S.A. Weaver, *John Fielden and the Politics of Popular Radicalism 1832–1847* (Oxford, 1987). Todmorden cotton master and high-profile radical.

H. Weisser, *British Working-class Movements and Europe, 1815–48* (Manchester, 1975).

J.H. Wiener, *The War of the Unstamped* (Ithaca, 1969).

J.H. Wiener, *William Lovett* (Manchester, 1989). Useful short biography of an important figure.

I. Wilkes, *South Wales and the Rising of 1839* (Beckenham, 1984).

Richard Williams, *The Contentious Crown: Public Discussion of the Monarchy in the Reign of Queen Victoria* (Aldershot, 1997). Useful for republicanism.

M. Winstanley, 'Oldham radicalism and the origins of popular Liberalism, 1830–52', *Historical Journal* 36 (1993), 619–43. Extension of the Foster debate (see above) and an argument for long-run continuity.